The Knights of Avalon

Happy Landings —
Dave Johnston

Dedication

To water planes and their pilots and the people who love them.

First published in 2004 by:

Horizon Line Press
77 North River Drive
Roseburg, Oregon 97470 USA

Copyright © David L. Johnston, 2004

All rights reserved. With the exception of quoting brief passages for the purposes of review, no part of this publication may be reproduced in any form without prior written permission from the Publisher.

While the information in this book is true to the best of our knowledge, the Publisher disclaims any liability incurred in connection with the use of this data or specific details.

Library of Congress Cataloging-in-Publication Data

ISBN 0-9749426-0-X

Printed in the United States of America

Contents

Acknowledgments
Prologue

Part I - The Island — 13
    First Flight
    The Hollywood Connection
    Dining on the Terrace

Part II - Water Striders — 43
    Early Days, Glenn Martin, Donald Douglas
    William Boeing - The Post Office and Pan Am
    Rugged and Handsome - The Grumman Goose
    The Last Winged Sikorsky
    Charles Blair

Part III - The Knights of Avalon — 83
    Dick Probert
    Nancy Ince-Probert
    Jugs Burkhard
    Clarence Jasper
    Fred Pierce
    Warren Stoner

Part IV - Adventures in Paradise — 141
    A Dock Boy Morning
    Docking 881
    The Glass Bottom Boat
    Bruce The Barracuda
    Tricksters

Epilogue
Bibliography
About the Author

Acknowledgments

Grateful recognition is extended to the following superstars who all helped in many ways with the publication of this book:

Janet Johnston
Steve & Diana Brown
Dottie Burkhard
Lloyd Burkhard
Russel & Frances Burkhard-Sasaki
Sybilla Cook
Brian Dawes
Gary Fisk
Georgia French
Warner & Judie McIntyre
John Phelps
Alice Pierce
Irene Pierce
Dick & Nancy Probert
Sandy Putnam
Alice Stoner
Chuck Stoner
Neal & JeanMarie Robertson
Mike Stansbury

Photographic Credits: Dottie Burkhard; Russel & Frances Burkhard-Sasaki; Brian Dawes; Gary Fisk; Susan Lurvey - Experimental Aircraft Association - Oshkosh, Wisconsin; Warner & Judie McIntyre; Adriana Paradisi - Santa Catalina Island Company; Jeannine Pedersen - Catalina Island Museum; John Phelps - Twin Harbor Enterprises - Catalina; Alice Pierce; Dick & Nancy Probert; Sandy Putnam; Alice Stoner; and Chuck Stoner.

Located just 22 miles off the southern California coast, Santa Catalina Island is 21 miles long and 8 miles wide at its widest point. The isthmus at Two Harbors is approximately ½ mile wide.

Avalon is the only incorporated city on the island - it is approximately 1 mile square and has a year-round population of about 3,000 people. During the summer tourist season the number multiplies to around 3 or 4 times this amount.

Prologue

Personal Involvement

So, why am I writing this book? After years of regaling people with island aviation stories at cocktail parties, and hearing the "you should write a book" comment from everyone, I have finally followed through with it. Aviation historian Gary Fisk in particular, urged me to put my stories on paper, and has been an ardent source of both support and materials.

I had no way of knowing at the time that I was going to be a very small part of a magical, romantic, and historical era during the years that I worked for an airline on Santa Catalina Island located just off of the southern California coast. The island itself has a romantic past—it was home to Indians, pirates, smugglers, and it possesses an interesting array of flora and fauna due to its isolation from the mainland.

With only a dim understanding at that time of the 50 years of aviation tradition on the island since 1912, I began work for Avalon Air Transport in the summer of 1962 as a dock boy. AAT later changed its name to Catalina Air Lines and it operated between five and seven (depending on which year you counted) Grumman Gooses, three Douglas DC-3's, a Sikorsky S-43, and one Sikorsky VS-44A 4-engine flying boat. Each of these aircraft was flown by an Air Transport rated pilot with a Multi-engine, Sea rating. To qualify for this classification, it takes years of flying in the most difficult conditions to earn your "water-wings." These water pilots - these "Knights of Avalon," are the reason for this book. Several of their stories follow. All "Knights" require a supporting cast, therefore, stories are also included about the aircraft, the mechanics, stewardesses, reservation agents, counter and ramp personnel, and dock boys who served these knights.

We all have dreams about paradise, where we are whisked away in ultimate style to the warm climes and tropical breezes of a magical island, with palm trees, a beautiful blue bay, and boats in the harbor with puffy white clouds overhead. The magic, romance, and adventure of those dreamy times are captured in the picture of a luxurious flying boat - winging its way to an island of intrigue. Why is this picture so dreamy - you ask? Because we didn't have a chance to participate! Flying boats were very few in number, and they were enjoyed by few people - for a very short time.

Most inventions go through a period of assimilation into a culture —we never really had a chance with this one. Inventions usually begin with a few costly examples, and, over time, progress to the point where they become commonplace and people become bored with them. The automobile, television, freeways, jet travel, and moon shots, are all inventions that follow this pattern. With seaplanes and amphibians, we never gave them a chance to increase in number and reduce in price. Paradise lost. This book will illuminate a second chance to view this lost era and the fascinating world of these amazing ships and the people who designed and flew them.

Motivation

Three recent events prompted the creation of this book. First, in 1997, there was a reunion in the southern California town of Avalon on Catalina Island. The public and any employees who had worked for any airline that served the island were invited. Hundreds of people showed up: former pilots, mechanics, office personnel, reservation and ramp agents, dock boys, former passengers and simply people who walked in from the street. The water pilots and their aircraft were the biggest draws. Everyone who attended fully enjoyed themselves and realized that they had been very fortunate to be around both the pilots and the planes.

The second motivation was a tragedy that occurred close to home. About 20 miles from my home in Oregon lived a man who had achieved almost unbelievable feats with aircraft. His name was Marion

Carl. He served in WWII as a Marine fighter pilot in the South Pacific. He became the Marine's first air ace; fighting at Guadalcanal, at the battle of Midway Island, and in the Solomons. After the war, he became a test pilot where he proceeded to set world speed and altitude records for the Marines, became the first Marine to be rated to fly helicopters, and the first to land a jet on an aircraft carrier.

All of these accomplishments were performed before he had reached the age of 33. One of my favorite stories about this man occurred during an air show in the late 1940's at the Patuxent River Naval Air Station in Maryland. He was flying a Grumman Bearcat - still one of the hottest performing propeller planes around. The Bearcat was fired off the deck catapult of the brand new aircraft carrier USS *Benjamin Franklin*. After this rocket launch, Carl would immediately pull straight up, lower the flaps, and land back on the deck of the flattop, all in one complete circle! He modestly stated: *"It was probably the shortest air show performance ever, but it was pretty spectacular."* He is widely regarded as one of the finest pilots who ever lived. The century just passed produced some stunning accomplishments by some rare individuals. We need to appreciate them before they are gone. General Marion Carl was killed by an armed intruder at his home in 1998.

The third motivating event occurred when I read Tom Brokaw's book *The Greatest Generation*. It profiled some of the outstanding people of the 20th century who had accomplished great things with little fanfare. I realized, like Tom, that time is running out, and thousands of this "greatest generation" are dying every single day. I also realized the need to recognize, celebrate, and learn from these extraordinary individuals who had set such high standards for lifetime accomplishments. This book attempts to do just that. All of the stories in this book are true. Only some of the names have been changed, to protect the guilty.

It is astounding to discover that it really is "a small world" - that the paths of people's lives cross in the most unique ways: in *The Knights of Avalon*, we will see that a small number of people flew a small number of aircraft for a short number of years, and we will see that they had a great effect on the world. Most of these seaplanes and amphibians no longer exist, a small number are now in museums. Many of the pilots are also gone. Now is the time to celebrate their contributions to our world. The people who designed, built, and flew during the romantic times described in *The Knights of Avalon* are real aviation pioneers.

First Trip in an Airplane

I was already 20 years old when I took my first ride in an airplane—it was to Catalina Island. I had been working up to it for a long time. Fifteen years prior, during World War II, my family's home was just underneath the flight path at the west end of the Torrance, California airport. Every day, we saw aircraft of all types rising into the brilliant blue skies, their unknown futures shimmering before them. I can even remember sometimes sneaking out of the house at night with my olive-drab army flashlight—signaling to any plane that might be flying overhead—to let the pilot know that I was with them in spirit.

We lived near the junction of the Pacific Coast Highway—Hwy 101—and Hawthorne Blvd. We were surrounded by airports and aircraft manufacturing plants. Douglas Aircraft and Northrup Aircraft Corporation had several major plants within a few miles and the airports at Torrance, Hawthorne, Long Beach, and Los Angeles all teemed with activity. The highway in front of our house carried a steady stream of military and aviation truck convoys of all sorts - including tanks, troops, airplane fuselages, wings, and tail sections.

During World War II, my twin brother and I were fascinated by aircraft. We had numerous silhouette airplane spotter cards (mostly Japanese aircraft - with some German) stuck to the wall in our bedroom. These cards were intended to be used by citizens to help watch for and identify enemy aircraft—and we both vowed to be the first to render this patriotic duty. Although my brother and I never saw any of the enemy, we had developed the habit of carefully scrutinizing anything that moved in the sky. Everything about airplanes excited and inspired us. We built models, read airplane books and magazines, and traced the magazine pictures to decorate our bedroom walls.

The years immediately following the war were also bustling with aviation activity around our house. The year 1947 was a perfect example of this exuberance. We saw the Northrup Flying Wing—forerunner to the Stealth Bomber—as it flew overhead. We heard the sonic boom as Chuck Yeager broke the sound barrier over the desert, and we saw Howard Hughes lift his big flying boat off the water on the only flight it ever performed.

The Hughes Flying Boat was dubbed the "Spruce Goose" by the press—although it had very little spruce in it. One particular brisk fall day in 1947, our father had taken my brother and me up to the top of a hill near our home. It was near San Pedro overlooking the Pacific Ocean and the Long Beach harbor. My father was a former race car mechanic and was therefore a fan of anything that was powered by an engine. So off we went to the top of the bluff to watch. On the hill with us were lots of other cars and people. I remember that all of the men wore hats, and one had a large camera on a tripod. Everyone seemed intent on watching an aircraft that was buzzing around in the harbor below. Suddenly, there was a great clamor from the assembled crowd. This small plane—we were a long way from the harbor below—had actually lifted off from the water! It wasn't until many years later that I found out we had witnessed the flying boat taking off on its one—and only—flight.

Our home in Torrance was located in a nearly direct line between Los Angeles International (LAX) and the airport on Catalina Island. From there, we were able to see the flight operations of United Airlines. They used Douglas DC-3's on scheduled flights back and forth to the "Island-in-the-Sky" airport (SXC) on Catalina Island. Every time the shiny silver, blue, and white aircraft would wing its way overhead, my brother and I would look up and say "there goes the Catalina plane."

Even with all of the influence of the '40 and '50's regarding aircraft in my blood, it still wasn't until 1961 that I took my first flight in an airplane. David Turner—a close friend and neighbor—told me that he was going to take a job for the summer on Santa Catalina Island. He was going to work for an airline that flew from Long Beach to Avalon, and he suggested that perhaps I should apply for a job there as well. So, that winter, I called Avalon Air Transport at Long Beach airport and booked a flight reservation to go to the island to apply for a job.

The Long Beach airport terminal was—and still is—a beautiful building, styled in the art-deco theme popular in the 1930's. The terminal is filled with visions of all the adventurous people who preceded me. After finding my way to the loading gate, I spotted a blue and white airplane. It was a high-winged, twin-engine Grumman Goose—with the registration number N322 proudly painted on the fuselage. It sat at a "funny" angle because it was a "tail dragger", and it had a small portable stairway on wheels bumped up against the single loading door near the tail of the ship. The weather was cool and the sun shining below that type of high thin scattered clouds that southern California is sometimes famous for in the winter. The ramp agent let us through the gate and we all loaded into this small ship.

The two-part entry door closed with a distinctive thump, the ramp agent yelled "clear" and the big radial engines smoked and roared to life—one at a time. This particular aircraft held nine passengers, including the lucky one sitting in the co-pilot's seat. The pilot was visible through the small, oval opening between the cabin and the cockpit. I could see that he had wild white hair under his cap, a bushy spread of mustache to match, and blue eyes. His cap was at a slight angle rather than squared away on his head. One pant leg of his trousers was in his flight boot, and the other was outside—he was a perfect example of a man who had great experience but was humble about it. This, my first pilot, I found out later, was an absolute classic gentleman named Clarence Jasper—"Jaz" for short. There is a mysterious quality about nicknames—or at least about people with nicknames. Nicknames can be complimentary, derisive or something in between. Having one usually indicates that the person has some depth of character. There is more to their past than meets the eye. This was certainly the case for Jaz.

We taxied out to the end of the runway for takeoff, and as Jaz "poured the coal to her" we lifted off over Long Beach—I was enthralled. The landing gear was retracted electrically at first, and then finished by hand cranking the last half dozen turns. Jaz made a quick check through a small observation port to verify that the wheels were completely up. The craft turned and headed toward the island—which was already in view—and the land began to slip away from beneath us as we proceeded out toward the Pacific Ocean. Many boats were visible in the Long Beach harbor below. A tanker was coupled to a large hose on-loading oil in mid-harbor, and a few pleasure craft were beginning to venture out into the winter white caps of the open ocean.

Flying over the San Pedro Channel, we saw the island become rapidly bigger as we approached. Jaz began talking into his microphone. I assumed that he was talking to someone in the small island town that was now visible on the coast below. It was exciting to see the palm-tree lined bay from above with its scattering of moored boats. Listening to one side of the radio conversation, it was apparent that something was amiss. We were not going to land in the normal spot—whatever that was—but we would look for a "better" location.

We turned away from the bay and flew along the rugged coast to the northwest for a minute or two. Then we turned back again toward the bay, which was now about 5 miles away, and Jaz began the decent. As the water rose up to meet us, I had a great revelation - we were going to land on the water! This was a complete surprise to me and I hoped that I was the only one who was surprised. As I scanned the other passengers, it was obvious that they understood that this was normal, so I eagerly began to look forward to the arrival. Since this was the off travel season, I was probably the only uninitiated "tourist" on the flight—the others were most likely islanders returning from some mainland shopping or other appointment.

For landing, Jaz headed us into the wind and reduced power until we were just a few feet above the top of a large swell. He reached up with his right hand and pulled both power levers full back - the engines reacted with slight rumbles as the rpm's dropped to idle. The bow of the ship was gently pulled up as the hull made contact with the top of the wave. The sound was like a fire hose against the side of a metal barn. We began skipping along the top of the swell and losing forward momentum at the same time. Finally, the ship lost enough speed to allow the pontoons to settle and we completed the transition "from a bird to a fish."

During the touchdown and run on the water, the spray completely covered the aircraft. I was excited. The noise from the engines quieted and the sound of the water was preeminent for a second or two. When the ship had wallowed to a stop, Jaz opened his pilot's cockpit side window for ventilation, and then increased the power in both engines to begin our water taxi toward the bay. My side of the ship was facing the rugged coastline of the island, and I could see that there was no beach at all, only wild waves dashing up against the sheer cliffs that make up this Pacific island.

Our taxi time to Avalon Bay took about 10 minutes, the same amount of time that we had been airborne, and I was enjoying the ride until I noticed that the seam between the fuselage and my window was leaking! I looked around to see if anyone else had a leak around their window, too. There didn't appear to be anyone else looking at their elbow for wetness like I did. Finally, we rounded Casino Point at the northwestern edge of the bay and finished our lengthy taxi to the float attached to the side/end of the Avalon Pleasure Pier.

At the water end of the pier was a cluster of three enterprises. The Avalon Fish Market faces the shore and it has the Avalon Harbor Master's office stacked on top of it facing the ocean. Both were painted in what is locally known as "Pleasure Pier" green. In front of this double stack sat the blue and white AAT airline office that overlooked the bay and faced the ocean.

We deplaned, climbed up the blue and white ramp and wound up at the top of the pier, on a bright, sunny and windy day. All of the

Avalon Bay in the winter season. The Casino building is at the top, in between is the old steamer pier—which was removed in the 1970's, with the passenger ship "Magic Isle" approaching the green Pleasure pier. The Avalon Air Transport floats for Grumman Gooses can be seen to the right of the Harbor Masters' office at the water end of the Pleasure pier.

passengers and the plane's cargo—luggage, mail, and freight—headed down the pier toward Eric's hamburger stand. There, our pilot, Jaz, had just purchased an ice-cream cone which he was leisurely consuming. I was impressed that he displayed all this gentle ease after "saving our lives" in the open sea landing and taxi ride. His ability, grace, and his dynamic presence as a positive force of nature still lives with me to this day.

After spending a couple of hours successfully completing my interview and checking out the small town for next summer's prospects, it was time for me to check back in with the AAT office for my return flight to the mainland. It is a good thing that I did this somewhat early. The Goose that we had arrived on that morning had immediately returned to Long Beach. It was the only flight to have made it in and out of Avalon Bay all day. The winter sea conditions were too rough for any other pilots to land on the water that day. The net result of this experience was that what may have been a routine flight to the pilot, was the experience of a lifetime to this traveler.

For the return trip to the mainland, the airline personnel loaded us into a Volkswagen bus-taxi and we began to drive out of the one square mile town of Avalon. Almost immediately, we began climbing the side of the canyon where we encountered a control gate which required a magnetic gate card for opening. Once through the gate, we continued climbing along a one lane road lined with eucalyptus trees until we were at the top of the ridge that runs down the spine of the island. This ride, with its vistas and small valleys, reminded me of what California must have been like before anybody lived there. It was wild and beautiful with many trees, bushes, and views that would make any Chamber of Commerce member ecstatic. I found out later that we were getting a "free" inland tour—they charge the regular tourists for this scenic trip. This bus ride took nearly 30 minutes, along approximately 10 miles of narrow - winding road. No other traffic was encountered. Magnificent views of the Pacific Ocean, the white mainland cliffs of Palos Verdes, and the island itself displayed themselves for us along this ridge line drive.

The control tower at SXC.

Finally, the bus made the turn into the parking area next to a cluster of buildings that make up the Santa Catalina airport. This airport is known by at least four different names including: Catalina Airport, the "Airport-in-the-Sky," SXC (the international three-letter identifier for this airport), and simply as "the hill." Once we disembarked from the bus, on the left side we could see a large hanger and on the right was a control tower in the Mediterranean-Spanish (tile and stucco) architectural style that is prevalent on Catalina Island. On the ramp a parked Avalon Air Transport Douglas DC-3 was waiting.

Luggage and mail were loaded and then we climbed aboard. Upon entry, the deck angle seemed even steeper than the one on the Goose, and there were lots more seats, too. After latching our seat belts, we taxied to the northeast end of the runway and turned around for takeoff. The runway at SXC has a high point in the middle which means that you can only see your end of it but not the other end.

The ground falls steeply away from the runway surface at both ends, creating instant clearance between the ship and the planet. Both of these features combine into an interesting group of sensations for the passenger—not to mention the pilot. It is a bit like unexpectedly flying over the rim of the Grand Canyon in a helicopter. Our return from the top of the island, over the channel and back to Long Beach was appropriately lit by the sun setting in the west—peeking from under the high-thin clouds—and lighting up the golden wave crests 1500' below. I had taken my first flight and had encountered both classic aircraft and an absolutely classic aircraft pilot.

Catalina Air Lines Grumman Goose registration number N328 makes a winter approach for landing in Avalon Bay in the mid-1960's. With flaps down, she is trying to land as close to shore as possible to avoid the rougher water outside the shelter of the harbor. This landing style was known as the "canyon approach" where the pilot flew back up into the canyon behind the town of Avalon, returned over the town itself and landed right next to the Green Pleasure Pier. The winter seaplane docks can be seen extending from the east side of the pier.

PART I — The Island

First the earth cooled, then dinosaurs came, and Santa Catalina Island rose from the sea.

- David Johnston

Islands have an intriguing, almost mystical air about them that lures people. This magical aura probably exists from the time when humans first saw that silhouette on the horizon and wondered what was there. Isolated from the masses, island plants and animals develop distinct characteristics.

During my first airplane ride in a Grumman Goose to the island, I had the distinct impression that there was a lot of history and tradition behind this short trip from the mainland. In fact, Southern California was the perfect setting for the fledgling aviation industry at the beginning of the 20th century. The first flight ever from the mainland across the channel to Avalon Bay was flown by the aviation pioneer Glenn Martin in May, 1912. The 25-year-old aviator had constructed his own plane in an abandoned church in Santa Ana on the mainland and then flew it from Newport Beach to Avalon Bay. He had originally built his ship as a land plane but, just for this flight, he replaced the wheels with a skiff belonging to a friend. The flight covered 33 miles in 37 minutes in this home-built airplane. It was the longest over ocean flight at that time. In a Los Angeles Examiner article dated May 11, Martin is quoted as saying *"I was confident, had no fear; trip was great joy."*

Two witnesses to this event were small boys in Avalon who later became prominent citizens, Herb Wegmann and Johnny Windle. They were thrilled along with the rest of the town when Martin landed in the bay and taxied onto the south beach upon arrival. They saw Martin climb out of his ship dressed in his three piece suit and wearing an inner tube for a life jacket. Herb Wegmann ultimately became the Avalon Post Master, and Johnny Windle later took over the newspaper dealership from his father.

Exactly twenty five years later in 1937, Glenn Martin would return in another flying boat of his design—the Martin M-130 *China Clipper*. By this time, Martin's flying boats had set many world records flying across the Pacific for Pan American Airways. Herb Wegmann was in charge of this Silver Anniversary event. A parade was held to welcome this magnificent ship and its designer, with the whole town turning out, many wearing costumes from the 1912 era. After the celebrations, when the *China Clipper* returned to the mainland, Herb Wegmann was given an honorary ticket to fly to Newport Beach, a distance of approximately 35 miles.

The first flight in history to Catalina Island was by Glenn Martin in May of 1912. The "Hollyhill House" built in 1890 still stands on the hill today.

Part I — The Island

Glenn Martin refueling his ship on the beach in Avalon. Note the inner tube that he used for a life preserver.

A Shriner attending a convention in Avalon autographs Martin's ship. Herb Wegmann stated that Martin "was not amused."

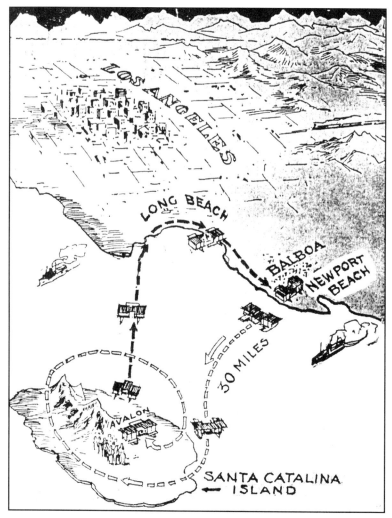

This Los Angeles Examiner *map shows the route that Glenn Martin flew in 1912. The structure in this artist's sketch that resembles a two car garage is Martin's seaplane.*

This historic 1912 flight was just one early high point in an amazing sequence of cross-channel pilots and aircraft that have enriched the island mystique. Over the past century, planes and pilots have mingled on Santa Catalina Island with the glitter of famous personalities from Hollywood and the world of aviation. Aviation

Glenn Martin taxiis for takeoff on his return to the mainland. A patch that had been placed on one of the pontoons came off during this run causing some concern for landing on the other side—but all was well. Note the glass bottomed rowboat at left.

pioneers, Hollywood moguls, and business entrepreneurs all flocked to the sunny climate of Southern California. This combination spurred spectacular growth in aviation, movies, and in business as each enriched and encouraged the other.

The Hollywood Connection

In 1891, the wealthy sons of western stagecoach tycoon General Phineas Banning purchased the island of Catalina. They followed Portuguese explorer Juan Cabrillo, the King of Spain, Mexico, and a succession of rich and famous people who have owned Catalina Island. William Banning and his brothers immediately began to develop the town of Avalon as a resort. Housing lots were sold inside the city limits of Avalon, hotel construction began and the Catalina Island Golf Club was established. This golf course is one of the oldest in the United States. When the Golf Club was first constructed in 1892 it had only three holes - by 1929, it had 18 holes. The world famous Bobby Jones Invitational Tournament was hosted there from 1931 until 1955. In Avalon Bay, the Bannings employed glass bottomed row boat rides for tourists to observe the unique marine gardens of the island. By 1896, the Banning brothers had formed the Santa Catalina Island Company to control the development of the land outside of the city limits. Unlike the rest of the island, the City of Avalon is incorporated and is not owned by a private individual or company. The city is approximately one mile square — with about one-half of that extending out into the ocean. This allows for City control of a very valuable resource — the harbor and its moorings.

Meanwhile, back across the San Pedro Channel, the movie industry was just getting started. By 1911, Thomas H. Ince, silent film producer and director, moved his motion picture production company from New York to a ranch he had purchased in the Santa Monica mountains just outside of Hollywood — "Hollywoodland" back then. His several thousand-acre ranch near Pacific Palisades, became known as *Inceville*, and it was the model for virtually all modern film production studios. Thomas was quick to innovate and he used the latest technology in his movie productions. He was especially fond of the airplane and began using stunt pilots to spice up his movie shorts of bathing beauties. Later, Thomas Ince's son would live in Avalon, and his granddaughter would play a very important role in Catalina Island aviation as a record setting stewardess. In 1912, famed early director DW Griffith filmed a movie on the island. By 1919, 80% of all of the world's film production companies had moved to Southern California for the same reason that had attracted the pioneers in the aircraft industry — a sunny climate. Following World War I, the movie industry, the public's fascination with airplanes, and many former fighter pilots — turned barnstormer — all merged in Southern California with great effect.

Thomas Ince filmed the movie *Civilization* in 1915 which had several scenes shot on Catalina. By coincidence, a major fire broke out in Avalon. His film crew captured the scenes of this devastation and Thomas used some of the footage in his production when it was released. In an interesting side note, Thomas Ince's premature death in 1924 still stirs up controversy. His life was cut short following a party put on by millionaire publisher William Randolph Hearst. During an interview with Ince's granddaughter Nancy Ince-Probert, I heard the following description of events. Hearst held a birthday party aboard his yacht for Thomas Ince's 42nd birthday. The guest list included Hearst's mistress - film star Marion Davies, actor Charlie Chaplin, and a jazz band among others. In addition, Hearst wanted to talk to Ince about helping to manage Miss Davies' career because Hearst was getting into trouble trying to do it himself. Ince went to the party on the yacht alone because one of his sons was ill and Mrs. Ince had to stay at home to care for him.

During the yacht party near San Diego, Thomas Ince's ulcers acted up (even though this was prohibition, there just possibly may have been alcohol involved) and he had to be hospitalized. A railroad train car was hired and he was transported from San Diego back home where he ultimately died of a heart attack. Many people believe that this was brought on by the partying, drinking, and his existing ulcers. All of the ingredients for scandal were present: rich people, movie stars, adultery, and the Prohibition Era of the Roaring 20's.

Glossing over the facts and fueled by Hollywood's penchant for gossip, "tinseltown" reporters followed several different storylines. One version goes like this. Hearst was jealous of Chaplin over Davies and he shot Ince by mistake. This was supposedly witnessed by budding gossip columnist Louella Parsons whose career suddenly blossomed following the cruise. It is even said that this mystery is the plot behind the novel written by Patricia Hearst (William Randolph Hearst's granddaughter) entitled *Murder at San Simeon*. According to Ince's granddaughter, in spite of many conspiracy theories, Internet web-site speculations, and even a movie - *"The Cats Meow,"* there is no evidence of foul play or scandal in the Hollywood tradition.

After World War I, there was an explosion of growth and exuberance in America, and it flowed all the way to Catalina Island. Freed from the specter of the "War to end all Wars," America was just beginning to enjoy "America's Century," and an entrepreneurial spirit coursed through the veins of society. For example, Charlie Chaplin, a member of Thomas Ince's birthday cruise, had a half-brother named Syd Chaplin. Syd formed Chaplin Air Line in 1919 with service to Catalina. It was the third scheduled airline passenger service operating in the entire country. The world's first airline service began in 1914 between St. Petersburg and Tampa, Florida. The second was just four months earlier than Chaplin's, between Seattle and Victoria, B.C. using a very early Boeing seaplane—the Boeing B-1.

Chaplin began operations on the 4th of July 1919, with Syd's pilot Art Burns—a former Navy Lieutenant—flying a Curtiss MF *Seagull* flying boat. This was a single engine biplane that carried three people. The first flight carried movie star Edna Purviance and some newspapers. Syd Chaplin and Art Burns operated this mainland to

Early film star Edna Purviance delivers newspapers to Avalon in 1919. Contacts with Hollywood personalities were natural for Syd Chaplin because, like his more famous half-brother, Syd was an actor. Later, he starred in the 1925 stage production of Charlie's Aunt, and performed in films until the mid-1950's.

Catalina route daily for two months during the height of the summer 1919 travel season. Both the airplane and the airline were later taken over by Pacific Marine Airways.

During that same year, an event of major consequence in modern Catalina history occurred when William Wrigley, of chewing gum fame, purchased the island. It should be noted that the City of Pasadena and its close neighbors, was home to most of the wealthy citizens in southern California. The Banning family, the Wrigleys, General George Patton (who met his future wife in Avalon), millionaire Henry Huntington, Zane Grey, and a Professor of zoology named C. F. Holder. These wealthy neighbors from Pasadena and San Marino all liked to vacation (and many owned homes) in Avalon and,

Syd Chaplin and his pilot Art Burns in the summer of 1919. Passing in the background is a paddle-wheel glass bottomed boat. Zoology Professor C.F. Holder of Pasadena vacationed regularly on Catalina. He was the first to put a glass panel in the bottom of a row boat which was used in Avalon Bay in 1886. In 1898, Holder and some associates created the Tuna Club in Avalon.

Both aircraft and swimsuit designs have changed since the 1920's but the allure is still the same.

because William Wrigley so throughly enjoyed his vacation trips to the island, he bought it.

In addition to Wrigley Gum, the Wrigley Building, and Wrigley Field, William also owned the Chicago Cubs baseball team. Beginning in 1921, he brought the Cubs to the island for their spring training baseball camp, which remained their spring home until 1951. It is hard to imagine what effect bringing in the Cubs had at this time. In 1921, although the Los Angeles Angels of the Pacific Coast League were in existence, there were no major league baseball teams west of St. Louis, Missouri. Baseball fans and Avalonites alike were extremely pleased. At the start of spring training, when the team arrived in Avalon, there would be a lively welcoming parade sometimes featuring riders mounted on Wrigley's Arabian horses from his ranch on the island.

One interesting story concerns an announcer from radio station WHO in Des Moines, Iowa who attended the Chicago Cubs spring training camp in Avalon. This reporter had convinced his boss each year for three successive years that he could do a better job of broadcasting the Cubs games during the regular season if he could see

A view of Wrigley's Chicago Cubs training field with the golf course in the background. This field was used from the 1920's to the 1950's.

the team develop over the course of the preseason. One year, while waiting for the cross channel weather to clear enough for the steamer to cross safely to the island, the radio announcer contacted a Hollywood agent for a screen test with Warner Brothers Studios. Things worked out well for the broadcaster—whose name was Ronald Reagan.

William Wrigley had many rich friends in business and in Hollywood. He wanted to show them a good time when he hosted them on his island. In addition, he was a very talented entrepreneur and he began looking to improve his small paradise just across the channel from Hollywood. When he began, the island had no sewage system, no paved streets, inadequate water and power supplies, and lots of rattlesnakes. He began improvements immediately, even bringing to the island wild boar to control the reptiles, and deer to enliven the landscape. Through the Santa Catalina Island Company or SCI Co., he expanded tourist facilities and activities. He created jobs for the islanders (Catalina Island Tile—once produced by a Wrigley company—is still very highly valued today), and actively marketed Avalon as a destination resort. Activity on all fronts began to pick up. The music industry even shone the spotlight on the island when Vincent Rose & Al Jolson wrote the popular song "Avalon" in 1919 and it became a big success when Bing Crosby recorded it the next year.

The rising popularity of the island and the desire by Wrigley to make it a pleasing place to visit was hampered by the lack of quick and reliable transportation. There were two methods of transportation to and from the island, ship or seaplane. Back then, travel by ship took several hours and sometimes, during storms, was impossible. Ship travel to the island was greatly enhanced in 1923, when Wrigley built the steamship "SS Catalina." It was 307 feet long and capable of carrying 1,963 passengers. One event that set the tone for the tourist experience for more than 30 years was the Miss Catalina speedboat greeting that was performed when the steamer arrived in Avalon. These wooden speedboats were designed and built on the island. Not only did the boats look fast—they were fast!

A fleet of Miss Catalina speedboats race out to greet the arriving steamer. They are towing "aqua-planers."

Each day, when the SS Catalina approached Avalon Bay, these beautiful craft would race out to greet the steamer and circle it a few times which added greatly to the passengers' first impressions of their visit. This alone was impressive, but the scene was enhanced by the addition of several bathing beauties waving a greeting from each boat to give the arriving passengers the proper atmosphere. The engines (Liberty V- 12's) for these speedboats were purchased from the US Navy when they became surplus from an old seaplane program.

Seaplanes were required for travel to the island because only a few land airports existed anywhere in the world — let alone Catalina. Other factors besides the lack of a landing field contributed to the slow growth of air transport to the island. All throughout the roaring 1920's, airplanes were rare, expensive, somewhat dangerous, and did not have many passenger seats. Ideally, airline operations had to have larger aircraft and a steady supply of passengers to stay in business. In spite of these difficulties, Pacific Marine Airways provided service to the island during the 1920's using Curtiss HS-2L four-seat, biplane flying boats. They then added two Loening Air Yacht amphibians which carried 6 to 8 passengers and cruised at 100 mph. Pacific Marine and its parent Aeromarine Company had an excellent safety record, never injuring a passenger. They touted the safety of their air service and compared it to surface ships by saying *"The Catalina Island trip, with land always in sight should operate on an equal* [safety] *standard, especially in view of the radio sending apparatus with which the craft is equipped."* By the mid-1920's, America began to experience a boom in the number of new airlines.

Founded in July of 1925, Western Air Express was one of the first successful major airlines. Western Air Express rapidly expanded its mail and passenger routes. In June of 1928, WAE added Pacific Marine Airways, which had been providing the air service between Wilmington, California and Catalina Island. With the purchase,

An early Curtiss "F" boat nosed up to the ramp near Abalone Point. In the distance, the old dance pavilion at Casino Point can be seen. When the new Casino Ballroom was built in 1929, the old structure was moved and became the basic shell for the Avalon Bird Park sanctuary.

A Western Air Express seaplane gets some engine maintenance at the dock while in the background, the SS Catalina *approaches the harbor.*

A Loening amphibian crosses Avalon Bay in 1929. This particular design was known as "the boot."

Western acquired Pacific Marine's three Curtiss HS-2L flying boats and also added a Sikorsky S-38 amphibian, a Boeing 204 flying boat, and two Loening amphibians. Western Air Express was the forerunner of Western Air Lines (and ultimately, TWA). At the time, WAE was the largest air transport system in the world—and Catalina Island was a part of it. This Mainland to Catalina route was later taken over by the Wrigleys, who began their Wilmington-Catalina Airlines Ltd. in 1931.

Wrigley's efforts to develop his island, as well as the improving transportation picture, lured among others the famous writer of western novels Zane Grey to the island. Grey had experienced the delights of the island when he enjoyed his honeymoon there in 1906. Grey built his Hopi "Pueblo" styled home in 1924 on the west hill where it still stands overlooking Avalon Bay. Since Grey's death in 1939, the home has been used as a classic "getaway" hotel called the "Zane Grey Pueblo Hotel" or simply "Pueblo Hotel." To keep its charm, the hotel still has no telephones in the guest rooms and it has

The only Sikorsky S-38 in the fleet for WAE. It was the latest in style in 1928.

The Zane Grey "Pueblo" with its magnificent view. The new Wrigley mansion can be seen across Avalon bay.

retained the original swimming pool created in the shape of an arrowhead.

Other homes built included both William Wrigley's, and his son Philip's. William built the "mansion" on Mount Ada (named after his wife) in the east hills, while Philip built in the west hills overlooking the Bay. They also built the Hotel Atwater (named after William's daughter-in-law Helen Blanche Atwater), a factory to make the furniture for the Atwater, and had 1,000 "bungalettes" erected as summer housing for the Avalon visitors. With the addition of these new residents, the water supply became critical. As an example, the Hotel Atwater was originally built with 150 guest rooms, but only three bathrooms due to the water restrictions in place at that time. While water is still a concern today, supply has been augmented by a desalinization plant. In the years that followed, the Wrigleys built a

The beautiful Avalon Ballroom features the world's largest circular dance floor. On weekends, the SS Catalina steamer would arrive with nearly 2000 dancers in their evening wear ready to dance until midnight—when the steamer returned to the mainland. Live radio broadcasts brought the Big Band sounds to the rest of the nation.

grammar school, Avalon High School (GO Lancers!), and the Catalina Country Club. The Country Club facility was built just beyond the Chicago Cubs spring training practice fields. Some years, it served as a locker room and club house for the Cubs. At other times, it has been the golf course center and today it is the Country Club restaurant.

The year the Great Depression began, 1929, the $2 million "Casino Ballroom" located on Casino Point at the entrance to Avalon Bay was completed. This is a magnificent building, and it is the focal point of almost every photograph of the bay. At a height of 140 feet, this structure was the tallest building in Los Angeles County at that

Big Band leader Benny Goodman (back row, center with clarinet) poses with his orchestra on the Avalon steamer pier. The Wrigley mansion is at top.

time—it was the maximum height allowed due to earthquake restrictions. The building is called the "Casino Ballroom" even though it has always been used for ballroom dancing—it has never been used for gambling. Almost all of the famous "big bands" performed in the dome shaped ballroom setting, including Glenn Miller, Tommy Dorsey, Woody Herman, Kay Kyser, Bennie Goodman, Bob Crosby, and Russ Morgan. On weekends, all through the 1930's and even up until the 1950's, the Avalon radio station KBIG (now KBRT on the mainland) would broadcast live music on coast-to-coast radio from the Casino Ballroom in Avalon Bay.

The ground floor of the Casino building houses both the Catalina Museum and the beautiful world class, art-deco Avalon Theater—one of the first movie theaters in the world specifically designed for the new "talkies." This was at the edge of technology in those days—theaters with sound systems were a rare commodity and many film studios were reluctant to adopt sound. For example, even in 1932 the Academy Award for Best Picture went to *Grand Hotel* - a silent film production. The interior circular ceiling murals were designed by John Gabriel Beckman who had just finished designing the interior of the famous Hollywood landmark Grauman's Chinese Theater (know today as simply Chinese Theater). Later, Beckman worked in Hollywood as a set designer on such movies as *The Maltese Falcon* and *Casablanca*. Cecil B. de Mille, Louis B. Mayer, and Samuel Goldwyn all took advantage of the chance to travel in their private yachts across the channel to Avalon Bay, just to preview their new talking motion pictures.

Dining on the Terrace

One evening at his home overlooking beautiful Avalon Bay and the Casino Ballroom, Philip Wrigley was having dinner with some guests including David Renton — chief design architect and General Manager for the Santa Catalina Island Company. Over dinner the lack of reliable air transport to the island was discussed. During conversation it was

The Hotel Saint Catherine was built by the Banning family in 1918.

Hotel St. Catherine beach scene at Descanso Bay in 1938.

decided that Wrigley knew where he could locate an amphibian ramp, and Renton could design the airport terminal building. At dusk, they jumped into Wrigley's Deusenberg convertible and traveled overland to Hamilton Cove. This cove is the second cove north of Avalon Bay. To get there, you must first drive past Descanso Bay—a small bay—that featured the beautiful Hotel Saint Catherine.

It was dark by the time Wrigley's Deusenberg with her passengers made it over the hills from Avalon. As the spotlight was switched on to illuminate the beach below, Philip Wrigley pointed out the spot where he wanted the amphibian ramp to be located. When it was mentioned that there was no room to easily turn the planes around once they reached the top of the ramp, he knew of a remedy. Bringing his knowledge of the railroad with him from Chicago, Wrigley suggested a turntable for the top of the ramp. Just like turning a locomotive around in a roundhouse, all that a pilot had to do was taxi up to the turntable, where the plane could be rotated to face the sea for departure. Voila! The terminal building design fell to Renton—who drew up the plans using the Spanish style architecture that was the prevalent building style on the island at the time. Renton created a

An aerial view of Catalina Airport at Hamilton Cove—just past the Hotel Saint Catherine. A new rock jetty had just been added for protection from northerly sea swells. A Douglas Dolphin can be seen sitting on the turntable—ready for departure.

beautiful two-story terminal with a tower, upstairs offices, a waiting room, and a refreshments stand. When completed, the entire mini-airport created a storybook setting. The sea, the rugged cliffs, the small cove and tiny beach, the ramp with turntable, and the beautiful terminal with the garden and beach umbrellas, all contributed to the idyllic scene. While the Hamilton Cove terminal building no longer exists, the old hangar building has been moved to the interior of the island where it now stands at SXC.

Philip Wrigley was no stranger to aviation operations. Back in Chicago in 1917 when he was 22 years old, Philip had joined the US Navy. Captain William A. Moffett, a friend of his father's, was Commandant of the Great Lakes Naval Training Station, where Philip was stationed. Captain Moffett believed that aviation should play a large part in the future of the Navy and wanted to form a naval aviation unit at his station, but there were no federal funds for such an enterprise. Undaunted, Moffett was able to get several private financial backers from the Chicago area to back his plan, including William Wrigley. Eventually, Philip was named the head of the aviation mechanics school at the station, where he gained valuable experience in both flying boat operations and managing people. In 1925, Philip was elected president of the William Wrigley, Jr. Company of Chicago. The next year, he and three associates, Allan Jackson, vice-president of Standard Oil of Indiana; Marshall Field III; and Edsel Ford, invested in an airline called American Airways. By 1931, this airline would become United Airlines.

Another aviation friend of the Wrigley's was Donald Douglas, the owner of Douglas Aircraft. Douglas frequently traveled to Catalina on his 75' motor schooner *Endymion*. During one visit with Wrigley in Avalon, he decided that he would design and build the perfect amphibian aircraft for Wrigley's Hamilton Cove operation, the Douglas "Dolphin." These three friends—Philip Wrigley, David Renton, and Donald Douglas—brought together the cove, ramp, turntable, terminal building, and finally, the airplane to form a new company—Wilmington-Catalina Air Lines. The terminal was dedicated in August 1931, named "Catalina Airport," and served as

Uniformed members of the Chicago Cubs baseball team in front of a Douglas Dolphin on the turntable in the 1930's.

the island base for Wilmington-Catalina Airline, Ltd. On the mainland, the departure point for the Dolphins was adjacent to the Catalina Steamship terminal in Wilmington. From there, Wilmington-Catalina Air Lines continued to operate for the next ten years. The March 1941 issue of Flying and Popular Aviation noted this company as having *"the shortest airline* [route] *in the world"* with the world's largest landing strip (the Pacific Ocean). The article points out that not only was Wilmington-Catalina Air Line the shortest—serving two towns less than thirty miles apart—but also the safest airline, having flown the channel 38,000 times carrying more than 200,000 passengers with no accidents or injuries between 1931 and 1941.

When Wilmington-Catalina Air Lines took delivery of the newly completed Douglas Dolphin amphibians, demonstration flights were arranged for Avalon Bay. There, William Wrigley, Philip Wrigley, David. M. Renton, and Rogers Hornsby (Manager of the Chicago

With landing gear up, Wilmington Catalina Airlines' Dolphin is headed for Hamilton Cove.

Cubs), were waiting. The pilot asked the men on the pier *"Who wants to go?"* Philip Wrigley, Renton, and Hornsby all headed for the plane.

"Wait a minute!" cried William. *"Rog, you can't go."*

"Why not?" Hornsby asked.

"You're too valuable!" William responded.

Even though the Depression years put the brakes to the world's economy, movie stars and the very wealthy seemed to be insulated. During those years, the list of celebrities that frequently visited Avalon—usually on their expensive yachts—included such names as Charlie Chaplin, Paulette Goddard, Stan Laurel, Oliver Hardy, Richard Arlen—(a star in the very first Academy Award winning movie *Wings*), Johnny Weismuller, Edgar Rice Burroughs, and Errol Flynn. Flynn's 76' yacht *Sirocco* was party headquarters for years in Avalon Bay.

Winston Churchill with his marlin catch on the Green Pleasure Pier in Avalon.

Actress Paulette Goddard with a friend and Sid Grauman of Grauman's Chinese Theater are surrounded by Catalina tile work on a patio in Avalon.

Paulette Goddard and Charlie Chaplin in the afternoon sun on Crescent Avenue. They frequently visited Avalon on their yacht.

Olympic champion swimmer and "Tarzan" actor Johnny Weismuller with young Hollywood star Mickey Rooney tee it up at the Catalina Country Club.

Another film star with connections to Avalon was western movie actor Tom Mix. He starred in the Zane Grey film *Riders of the Purple Sage* and he owned and lived in a house just down the hill from Grey in Avalon. Tom was one of the first movie cowboys—you may recall seeing one of his movies in which he would whistle and his horse "Tony" would come to save him. Tom infuriated his neighbors in Avalon when he mounting an electrically lit sign on his house with his initials "TM" inside a diamond shape that glowed all over the neighborhood at night.

The Wrigley family had always been interested in horses, and in 1930 Philip built a horse ranch—El Rancho Escondido. He began with 24 palominos and later added Arabians to the ranch. The ranch is located on an old stage road that Philip had lined with eucalyptus trees. He also attempted to landscape around his ranch house but he met with some difficulties from imported animals. Earlier, Hollywood studios were responsible for bringing goats, deer and buffalo for movie productions on the island—*Mutiny on the Bounty* was filmed on the island in 1935. Even fencing could not keep the deer and buffalo, from munching the Wrigley-planted shrubs and flowers. Buffalo you say? The initial herd of 14 was brought to the island in the mid-1920's to film a western movie *"The Vanishing American"* a Zane Grey story, and were never removed. Around 200 of these animals remain on Catalina today, where they continue to root up plants while thriving in the island climate. Wrigley himself brought wild pigs from nearby Santa Cruz Island to help keep the rattlesnake population down.

Movie star visits drastically diminished with the coming of war. After December 7, 1941, World War II effectively sealed off the island as far as civilian air transport was concerned. Many Hollywood actors who were used to frequenting the island had to, for the most part, remain on the mainland for relaxation. The current crop of stars so affected included Humphrey Bogart, Lauren Bacall, John Wayne, and many actors from England - David Niven, Charlie Chaplin, Sir Laurence Olivier, Errol Flynn, and Ronald Coleman to name a few.

During the war, the armed forces virtually took possession of the island. A nearly finished airport being built by Wrigley in the interior—SXC—had logs placed across the runway early in the war to block unauthorized aircraft from landing. The US Army set up radar sites in the interior hills to watch for enemy aircraft (my brother and I were not alone in our vigilance), the US Navy held bombing practice at the west end of the island, and the Office of Strategic Services—the forerunner of the CIA—set up survival training camps at various points on the island. In addition, the US Coast Guard located a base at Two Harbors—at the isthmus of the island, and the Signal Corps also had installations. The Maritime Service - Merchant Marine set up Liberty Ship training at the Hotel Saint Catherine, Avalon Bay and later, at both the Hotel Atwater and the Island Villa.

Following the war, movie star visitors returned to enjoy the charms of the island. One character from the island was almost as notable as the stars he associated with—his name was Duke Fishman and he was prominent both before the war and after.

Henry Fonda, Duke Fishman, and Ward Bond help dispense "Duke" suntan oil on the pier in Avalon.

Both "Dukes" - John Wayne and Duke Fishman on the Pleasure pier in the 1960's.

Duke was a fixture on the island for over four decades. His physical fitness, positive demeanor, and his distinctive looks all contributed to his role as an icon for Avalon. Remember the TV ads for Mr. Clean the household cleaner? These featured a muscular, shaved headed, genie type of character with an earring who promised to provide strong cleaning power. Duke was the prototype for this character. He was born in the Philippines in 1906, and had a varied career in show business playing bit parts in famous movies such as Mutiny on the Bounty (1935), The Ten Commandments (1956), Spartacus (1960), and The Planet of the Apes (1968). He also made character actor appearances on several TV shows. In Avalon, Duke was seen every summer on the beach, along Crescent Street, and on the piers—especially whenever the steamer arrived or departed. Wearing his trademark red lifeguard shorts with his sea captain's hat slightly askew, he was the official Avalon greeter, head lifeguard, and schmoozer with the stars. He posed for tourist pictures, took pictures, and cleaned the beach in the mornings—in short, he was everywhere. Sadly, Duke passed away in 1977. He is still missed.

From Glenn Martin's unbelievably courageous beginning in May 1912, to the high tide of celebrity influence, many fascinating and famous people and events provide a rock-solid foundation for the future sea/air adventures on the magic island of Catalina.

PART II — Water Striders

"Seldom was any industry advanced as rapidly as aviation."

- Igor Sikorsky

Early Days

The rapid transition from the fragile wood, fabric, and wire airplanes to the sleek, modern transcontinental airliners we take for granted today was an exciting period in our history. There are a few key players who have helped us to leap over oceans, straddle continents, and forge our modern world. Over the past century, we have experienced the rapid development of many inventions - the telephone and automobile are excellent examples. Most recently the personal computer, like the car and phone before it, has shown explosive growth and change over the last twenty years. The advances in airplane design have enjoyed an equally dynamic time. It took a little time for the wings of progress to get under way but once begun, progress came rapidly.

The accomplishment of the Wright brothers' first flight on December 17, 1903 fired the imagination of a man named Glenn Curtiss, who in October 1907, along with Alexander Graham Bell and others, formed the Aerial Experiment Association. They set up an airplane flight school to train themselves and others to pilot these new creations that they were constructing. In 1911, Curtiss attracted the interest of the US Navy when he landed his "hydroaeroplane" next to the cruiser USS *Pennsylvania* that was moored in the harbor at San Diego, California. By 1914, Curtiss had created a pusher biplane that co-starred in several episodes of the silent film serial *The Perils of Pauline*. The connections between aviation, the military, and the film industry had begun.

The Wright's first flight occurred just one hundred years ago from a lonesome beach using a plane that was basically a kite powered by a small engine. It is hard to believe now, but the public didn't really take notice of the new ability to fly until six years later in 1909, when the Wrights flew their craft over the Hudson River in full view of the Manhattan Island office workers in New York City. This event succeeded in gaining the public's attention—but the real progress was yet to come. It is said that "war is the mother of invention," and certainly World War I brought many advances in the size, uses, and abilities of aircraft. However, some of the greatest advances and achievements occurred in the twenty short years between the two World Wars.

This frenetic time between the two World Wars is referred to as the *Golden Age of Aviation*. The explosion of interest and growth came in a variety of forms. National Air Races were held for the first time in January 1919, at Dominguez Field just south of Los Angeles. Flight records of all kinds were broken almost every day, barnstorming stunt pilots traveled the country giving the first airplane rides to citizens who were enjoying the good life of the 1920's. Mammoth lighter than air ships like the *Graf Zeppelin* and the *Hindenburg* began to roam the skies, and independent builders began to tackle the wide-open vistas of aircraft design. With the world war over, military aviation didn't really have much to do, so they combined their aircraft and pilots with the Hollywood movie industry to make several films which kept aviation in the public eye and also helped with pilot recruiting. Newspapers, philanthropists, and businesses offered various prizes for aviation firsts. Distance and endurance records were pursued by military and private pilots alike. The Army, the Navy, Charles Lindbergh, Amelia Earhart, Howard Hughes, and many, many others all accomplished great feats during this time between the world wars.

Back during World War I, the Navy took advantage of Glenn Curtiss's design experience and contracted with him to build seaplanes for them. The most popular Curtiss design was the HS-2L of which more than one thousand were produced. Because of his contributions, he is considered "the father of naval aviation." Curtiss alone could not manufacture the quantities of seaplanes that the Navy required, so other aircraft factories were utilized, including Boeing in Seattle, and Loughead (later changed to Lockheed) in Southern California.

It is interesting to note that one of the draftsmen working for Lockheed was John K. Northrup, who became one of the most influential aircraft designers of the 20th century. During the second World War, Lockheed went on to create the famous "Skunk Works" that has been responsible for such designs as the first American jet fighter - the P-80 "Shooting Star," the U-2 spy plane, the SR-78 "Blackbird," and the F-117 "Stealth" fighter. Now, in the 21st century, the Lockheed/Martin Company (the same Glenn Martin who first flew into Avalon Bay) is building the modern Joint Strike Fighter (JSF).

Despite the military aviation advances of the first World War, the extent of commercial aviation was extremely limited. Passenger trips were expensive, dangerous, and the lack of infrastructure made it inconvenient. For several years during the "Roaring Twenties," virtually no air passenger traffic existed. The lack of higher performance aircraft engines limited the lifting power and, therefore, the number of seats in which to haul enough people for an airline to make a profit. Safety was also a major concern. For example, the US Government began hauling the mail by aircraft in 1919. By 1925, of the original 40 pilots hired by the Post Office Department, over 75% of them had been killed in airplane crashes. Smarting from this dismal record, the Postal Department opened up the air mail business to private contractors. This move provided potential air carriers with a steady source of revenue that could be combined with the carrying of passengers to hopefully make a profit. This single act of government subsidy signaled the dramatic beginning of a new era. It basically gave birth to the commercial airline industry in the United States.

In the same tradition as the Pony Express, the Trans-Continental Railroad, and more recently the Interstate Highway System, the airline industry rapidly succeeded in spanning the continent, speeding progress, and in many ways bound the country together. Meanwhile, the American public had few reasons to go flying. There were few airfields—at that time they were just that—"fields"—mostly unpaved cow pastures. The average citizen couldn't fly because almost no airlines existed, costs were high, and flying was (accurately) perceived to be dangerous. Each of these obstacles would be removed over the next few years. To overcome the landing field problem, a large percentage of aircraft constructed in the late teens and twenties were amphibians and seaplanes, designed for landing on the water.

Glenn Martin

One young man who was inspired by the potential of the airplane was Glenn Martin. Martin is the man who flew his hand made wood and wire craft over the open water channel to Catalina in 1912. He was a former automobile dealer who had in 1908 set up a rudimentary aircraft factory to build his own designs in Santa Ana, California. By 1915, he was hired to perform aerial stunts using his two-place model "TT" in the Mary Pickford film, *The Girl From Yesterday*. During World War I, the Martin Company began design and production of twin-engine bombers for the US Army. It should be mentioned that the chief engineer for the bomber project was a 1914 graduate of M.I.T. named Donald Douglas.

As years progressed, the Martin Company continued to develop designs which ultimately resulted in the award of a contract by Pan American Airways for the Martin M-130 *Clipper*. When completed in October 1935, it was the largest aircraft that had ever been built in the United States. The M-130, was however, slow and costly. The interior cabin was normally set up with seats for up to 46 passengers, and it resembled an elegant small hotel with a range of 3,200 miles at an average speed of 150 miles per hour. For long flights, overnight sleeping berths with curtains were used, just like those on trains for land travel. A total of three of these seaplanes were built. They were named *China Clipper, Philippine Clipper, and Hawaiian Clipper*.

The owner of Pan American, Juan Trippe, was responsible for carrying the "Clipper" theme forward in his operations in a number of ways. He wanted to recreate the image of the glory days of sailing ships when large, fast ships plied the oceans of the world, carrying the

American flag to major ports around the globe. In addition to naming all of his ships' "clippers," his pilots wore dark blue and white uniforms and caps in the naval style, and were referred to as captains. This tradition concerning pilots continues to be used in virtually all airline operations today.

Using the Martin M-130, Pan Am officially began trans-Pacific seaplane passenger service in October of 1936. This first flight had only seven fare paying passengers, each paying a special fare of $3,000 for the inaugural flight from San Francisco. The flight actually began from the seaplane base which was located at that time on Treasure Island across the bay in Alameda. The final destination was Manila in the Philippines with stops at the seaplane bases in Honolulu, Midway Island, Wake Island, and Guam. The very first passenger ticket, number one, was issued to Mr. R. F. Bradley, the Manager of the Aviation Department of Standard Oil. This ticket is now housed at the Smithsonian Institute to emphasize the significance of this first passenger flight across the world's largest ocean.

A Pan American Martin M-130 heads for Hawaii passing over the not quite completed Golden Gate Bridge.

In 1937, Glenn Martin took his China Clipper off of the regular schedule to fly it on a special trip to Avalon Bay in commemoration of the 25th anniversary of his 1912 flight to Avalon in his home built craft. Note the welcoming citizens in 1912 period costume.

Hamilton Standard Propellers could alter their pitch for economical cruise settings which allowed the Martin M-130 to cover long, over-water routes in the mid 1930's.

Another traveler on this history making flight was first flight fanatic, Clara Adams. This lady had also been a first flight passenger on other famous flights: in October 1928, she had been the only female passenger on the inaugural flight of the *Graf Zeppelin* from New Jersey to Germany, and she was on board the 1931 flight of the huge German Dornier Do X flying boat from Rio de Janeiro to New York. Clara had paid the premium price of $3,000 for her first flight ticket but later, as the Pan Am trip across the Pacific became more commonplace, the round trip fare stabilized at about $1,400. These regular round trip flights across the Pacific were scheduled to depart about every ten days.

Donald Douglas

Philip Wrigley's friend, Donald Douglas, got an early start in aviation at the age of 24, when he was hired in 1915 as an engineer to design seaplanes for Glenn Martin. Five years later, he left to form his own company in Santa Monica, California and he proceeded to build it into a world leader. By 1924, assisted by draftsman John Northrup, the Douglas designed "Douglas World Cruiser" flown by US Army pilots, would circumnavigate the world. This flight of four aircraft left Santa Monica in March and returned after a total of 175 days. Of the four original craft that departed, one crashed in Alaska, one sank after ditching in the Atlantic, and two finished the around the world trip. One of these remaining ships is currently on display at the National Air Museum in Washington, D.C.

By 1925, Douglas had designed his first flying boat—it was a twin-engine biplane—to perform coastal patrol work for the US Navy. This experience is what led him to volunteer his services to Wrigley to design and build the perfect floatplane for Wrigley's Hamilton Cove operation, the Douglas "Dolphin."

The Dolphin was one of the world's first commercial executive transports and Douglas believed that he could market it to wealthy individuals who both needed and could afford this rugged, mini-airliner. However, because of the Depression, only seven Dolphins

A Douglas Dolphin is readied for turn around at Hamilton Beach.

were sold to (wealthy) individuals who used them for such tasks as commuting between home and work or to their summer homes. One owner, William K. Vanderbilt, stored his on the stern of his 265' oceangoing yacht for those quick trips to shore for supplies. Another owner, William Boeing, gives an interesting testimonial for this aircraft—he bought one. Because Boeing Aircraft (let alone any other aircraft manufacturers) had no aircraft of this class in production at the time, Bill Boeing purchased a Dolphin in 1934 for executive travel. This is akin to Michael Dell using an IBM computer. Today, this same aircraft originally purchased by Boeing is the only surviving Dolphin in existence. It is the last of its kind, and it has been restored and is now owned by Colgate ("Coke") Darden, a famous private collector of antique aircraft.

A total of 58 Douglas Dolphins were built between 1931 and 1934. Most of them were for the US Army, Navy, and Coast Guard, and two went to China National Aviation Corporation. The world speed record for amphibians was set using a Dolphin on May 15, 1935. The man who set the record was a pilot for Standard Oil Company and his name was Major E.E. Aldrin. He was the father of astronaut Buzz Aldrin. Although this speed record was a satisfying accomplishment, Douglas was now moving on to bigger and better designs. By 1936, the Douglas DC-3 was unveiled, which carried 21 passengers and was the prototype for commercial airliners to come. Today, the Boeing/McDonald-Douglas Company is a world leader in the design and construction of both passenger jets and unmanned combat air vehicles (UCAV).

William Boeing, the Post Office and Pan Am

The small, interconnected world of people who designed aircraft all seemed to know one another—and to inspire each other. Around 1914, Bill Boeing took flying lessons from the Glenn Martin Flying School in Los Angeles. By 1916, he had designed and built his first two-seat airplane and by 1919, his model C-700 was being used by the second airline ever formed in the United States. All of this experience combined with two major forces to skyrocket Boeing fortunes. Those two forces were the US Postal Service and Pan American World Airways. The Post Office needed to make a change in how the mail was transported across the country. In response to the number of pilots who were killed flying the mail, the US Congress passed the Kelly Act in 1925. This allowed the Government to hire mostly private contractors to carry the mail.

Immediately, Bill Boeing formed the Boeing Air Transport of Seattle, Washington and by 1926, he had produced the Boeing 40A which could carry not only the mail, but two passengers. Within two years, BAT was carrying 30% of all of the mail and passengers in the US. In 1930, BAT introduced a brand new service on its flights between San Francisco and Chicago—female cabin attendants. These ladies were all registered nurses who wore capes and had to swear that they would not marry while employed at BAT. It was during this time that BAT merged with several other companies and, together, they ultimately formed United Air Lines, Inc.

Where the focus of United Air Lines was domestic, Pan American Airways was international in scope. The owner of Pan Am was the dynamic businessman Juan Trippe. Through the early 1930's, Juan had been using two main suppliers for his amphibians and seaplanes, Sikorsky and Martin, but he had succeeded in alienating both of them. When Juan Trippe asked for bid presentations for a new "Super Clipper," a more advanced flying boat, both Sikorsky and Martin were so outraged from prior business dealings with Trippe that they refused to bid for his contract. Boeing won by default. The result was that Pan Am acquired the most luxurious airplane in the entire world complete with a dining salon, a spiral staircase, and a cocktail lounge. Everything about this ship was 1st class. Champagne, caviar, linens, and silver were all part of the ultimate in air-borne luxury.

The Boeing model 314 was first delivered to Pan Am in January of 1939 and by February it replaced the Martin M-130 on the main trans-Pacific run. As each of the Boeing 341s was completed, it was flown from the Boeing plant near Seattle, Washington to Astoria, Oregon at the mouth of the Columbia River. This is where the final sale and ownership transfer occurred. Why finalize the transaction in Oregon, you ask? Just as today, there was no sales tax in the state of Oregon, and on a purchase price of more than one-half million dollars per aircraft, there was a substantial advantage with this procedure. Only 12 of these big flying boats were built with 9 going to Pan Am and 3 to the British air line BOAC.

On December 7th, 1941, Pan Am's ships had several close calls in the Pacific. Imagine being a passenger or crew member flying into the teeth of World War II. Here is just one experience. Six days out of its home port of San Francisco, the Pan Am Boeing 314 *Pacific Clipper* piloted by Captain Robert Ford was just two hours from its scheduled arrival in Auckland, New Zealand when the crew received a radio transmission that the Japanese had attacked Pearl Harbor. Captain Ford stayed in Auckland for one week awaiting word on what Pan Am wanted him to do next. Headquarters in New York finally decided that the safest way to get the big bird home was to continue to fly West. Taking on a spare engine, parts, and tools, Ford and his crew left the passengers in New Zealand to wait for other transport and then flew the rest of the way around the world by way of Australia, India, Central Africa, South America, and then on to New York.

In Australia, Ford realized that they would need some money to purchase aviation fuel and food for the lengthy return trip to New York. With the help of a friendly banker in Gladstone, Australia, who advanced them enough cash to get them back to the United States, they began their flight to safety. Approaching Surabaya on the Island of Java, Captain Ford was intercepted by a flight of Dutch fighter aircraft who fortunately did not fire upon this unscheduled arrival. Upon landing just outside the harbor, the Boeing was met (at a distance) by a harbor launch filled with frantically waving personnel. They found out later that they had landed in the middle of a mine field and that the crew of the launch had been trying to wave them out of it!

After traveling for a month, the big Pan Am ship finally slid into the safety of New York Harbor. You can imagine the astonishment of the air traffic control officer at La Guardia Marine Terminal when he heard *"Pacific Clipper, inbound from Auckland, New Zealand, Captain Ford reporting."* The ship and its crew had flown for 31,500 miles, and a total of 209 hours flying time in order to avoid the war zones and arrive safely. It was the first, though unplanned, round-the-world flight by a commercial airliner; no one had ever done it before.

Throughout the war, the Boeing Clippers sported military colors and served the US Navy using an on demand schedule. In 1942, the BOAC *Berwick Clipper* was used to fly Winston Churchill to a war conference with President Roosevelt in Washington, D.C. During this trip, Sir Winston was allowed to "pilot" the big flying boat, and he was very impressed. He later wrote, *"I traveled in an enormous Boeing flying boat which made a most favorable impression on me... I took the controls for a bit, to feel this ponderous machine of thirty tons or more in the air. I got more and more attached to the flying boat."* In January 1943, President Roosevelt crossed the Atlantic in the *Dixie Clipper* for the famous Casablanca Conference. En route, he celebrated his sixty-first birthday.

His Special Assistant Harry Hopkins noted the effect of the flight on FDR in his diary. *"I sat with him, strapped in, as the plane rose from the water — and he acted like a sixteen-year-old, for he has done no flying since he was President. The trip was smooth, the President was happy and interested."*

In February 1943, the *Yankee Clipper* was completing a trip across the Atlantic from the US to Lisbon, Portugal with a large contingent of USO entertainers. Upon landing in the early evening, the big Boeing caught a wing tip and crashed, killing 24 of 39 passengers. Among the 15 survivors was a popular singer of the day, Jane Froman. She was severely injured, but was kept afloat by the ship's Fourth Officer, John Burns, whom she later married. This was the only Boeing 314 that was lost because of a flying accident in all of their years aloft.

Pan Am's Pacific routes had taken five years to design, test, and perfect, but they were to be abandoned almost overnight. Many factors combined to doom the transoceanic flying boat. World War II saw the construction of new, paved land bases all over the world. Rapid improvement in the aerodynamics of wings, fuselage design, and engine development, all contributed to the ascendency of the land-based multi-engine, long range transport. The last Clipper flight for Pan Am was flown in 1946 from Honolulu to San Francisco. Today, after very short careers, all 12 of the Boeing 314 Clipper ships are gone. Storms, accidents, and the scrap heap claimed these magnificent symbols of that magic era. One aluminum trim tab about three feet long is all that remains. There are plans to construct and display a replica of a B-314 as part of the Seattle Museum of Flight. It is currently scheduled to open in 2005.

Rugged & Handsome - The Grumman Goose

Born in the late 1930's, the Grumman "Goose" was one of the main forerunners of today's business aircraft. Following in the wake of the Sikorsky S-38 and the Douglas Dolphin, the Goose continued to capture the imagination of forward-looking entrepreneurs. Executive jets such as the LearJet, Cessna Citation, Sabreliner, and even Air Force One, can all track their origins back to these ships that were designed for luxury, versatility, and durability.

Leroy (Roy) Grumman, the founder of Grumman Aircraft, did not start at the top. After a hitch in the US Navy as a pilot (Naval Aviator #1216), Roy was hired in 1921 by Grover Loening who was designing his "Loening - Air Yacht" amphibian on the East Coast. Loening himself had an interesting career, as he had worked as Orville Wright's assistant at the Wright factory at Dayton in 1913. During World War I, Loening was the Chief Aeronautical Engineer for the US Army in San Diego. During prohibition, his successful Loening amphibians were the aircraft of choice for the bootleggers flying rum into the Miami area. Later model Loening Air Yachts were used by Western Air Express to fly a regular schedule from Los Angeles and Long Beach to Avalon Bay in the mid 1920's to early 1930's.

Roy Grumman's retractable landing gear and hull configuration, designed for Loening, was both rugged and provided low drag. This was because the wheels retracted flush with the side of the hull. With a good reputation established, Roy's designs were used by other manufacturers who were building scout and observation planes for battleships. These types of planes needed to be rugged, because they would be catapulted off a battleship, perform the mission, and upon return, they would be hoisted back onto the ship—ready for the next trip.

By 1929, Roy founded Grumman Aircraft Engineering Corporation in New York, (one member of the Board of Directors was Albert Loening - brother of Grover) and by 1933 his factory produced the J2F-"Duck." You might remember seeing the "Duck" featured in the 1971 movie *Murphy's War*, starring Peter O'Toole. In this amazing product of Hollywood's imagination, Peter O'Toole learns to fly within about 15 minutes. He takes off from the water, loops through clouds, and lands back on the water without shearing off a float. When his first solo is complete, he maneuvers up to the wharf, ties up the ship, jumps out of the Duck and wraps his arm around the radial engine—without getting burned!

In 1935, a syndicate of wealthy businessmen asked Roy Grumman's former employer Grover Loening about an aircraft that would suit their business purposes. Loening wasn't in a position to help, so he suggested Grumman, and the design of the G-21 (Goose) was begun. The syndicate had asked for this new design to include two pilots, 4-6 passengers, with a small galley, a bar, and even a lavatory in the rear of the cabin. Because most of these businessmen worked in the financial district on Wall Street in New York City, the Hudson River was very close to their offices. An amphibian was the perfect answer for flying from airports to the river and back.

The Goose was rugged and could land on almost anything—fresh or saltwater runways, and on paved or—more likely—rough dirt runways. As an example, one Goose (#48 out of 345 total) sported cactus-proof tires when it was sold to its original owners - some oilmen in Caracas, Venezuela. Some Gooses (the preferred plural for these ships) were even fitted with skis for operations on snow-covered landing strips.

In addition to the famous Grumman retractable landing gear, the G-21 design had another major advantage over any other amphibian in existence—the engines were mounted on the leading edge of the

The Grumman J2F-"Duck" displays the classic retractable landing gear and hull configuration that Leroy Grumman used in his famous amphibians. All of his "amphibs" were named after waterfowl.

The Grumman Goose continued the "air yacht" theme begun by the Grover Loening Aircraft Company in the early 1920's. By 1935, Leroy Grumman had produced the perfect combination for the wealthy Wall Street commuter.

wing. Prior amphibian designs had the engines mounted on the top of the wing, which added extra weight and extra drag. These unique Grumman features, flush-retracting wheels and engines that blended into the wings, provided a major step forward in amphibian aircraft design of the time. In fact, in the almost 70 years since the Gooses' debut, there has never really been a comparably priced competitor. The Grumman Goose was the first really modern, high-performance amphibian and it cost just $68,000 in 1937. The price today for one of these 50 to 60 year old ships is probably in the area of one million dollars—if you can find one.

Within five short months after flight trials for the Goose began, government certification was issued. By the end of the year, the first dozen ships were delivered to their owners. In the middle of the "Great Financial Depression," the purchase price was certainly not affordable to the masses and taking a look at the first few owners reveals that the Goose was a luxurious status symbol, to be used as an "Air Yacht" - sought after by those with financial prowess - who were to become the first aero commuters.

Here is a partial list of first owners of this new design:

Goose number   Owner

- 2   Henry Morgan - (Banking)
- 4   C.W. Deeds - (United Aircraft)
- 5   Col. McKormick - (Chicago Tribune)
- 6   Boris Sergievski - (Sikorsky Aircraft - test pilot)
- 7   P. Crosley, Jr. (Cars, refrigerators)
- 8   Asiatic Petroleum
- 9   Lord Beaverbrook - (British Newspaper owner)
- 12 Gar Wood (A World Champion Speed Boat racer who owned two Gooses)

The owner of the ninth Goose that was produced—Lord Beaverbrook—actually owned two Gooses, #9 and #49. Goose #49 provides a look at the typical history of a Goose. Shortly after purchase, Goose #49 was impressed into military service by the RAF in North Africa where it was sunk during war action at Benghazi on December 9, 1942. The fates of other Gooses can be tracked in numerous books, publications, and Internet websites (see the bibliography).

The histories of Grumman Gooses evoke sadness and wonder. Following are some sample final dispositions:

Goose #20 - crashed in Kodiak, Alaska on Christmas Day 1961.

Goose #51 - scrapped.

Goose #48, referred to above with the cactus-proof tires, eventually was put in service flying between the mainland and Catalina for Air Catalina during the 1970's. After #48's retirement, it was painstakingly restored in Florida, and then shipped in large sections aboard a Boeing 377 MG "Guppy" belonging to Erickson Air-Crane of Central Point, Oregon. This beautiful Goose is now on display with its original paint scheme at the National Air & Space Museum in Washington, D.C.

By the end of the first year of production, about 20 Gooses had been sold to individuals and businesses. By 1938, civilian purchases had dropped off, but with the winds of war blowing, every branch of the military began placing orders. Between 1938 and 1945, when the last Goose was manufactured, the US Navy ordered a total of 222 Gooses. Other armed forces also placed orders in the following quantities; US Army Air Corps - 26; US Coast Guard - 13 (for iceberg monitoring, etc.); Britain ordered 55 Gooses for the RAF through the lend-lease program; Canada (RCAF) - 56; France - 12, which were used mainly in Vietnam in 1950's with machine guns mounted in the passenger entry door; and Portugal - 12 Gooses which had their landing gear removed - and acted as armed flying boats - rather than amphibians. The versatility of the Grumman design is quite evident in this list of roles the Goose played during various conflicts, including: Aerial photo reconnaissance, officer transport, maritime patrol, air/sea rescue & ambulance, antisubmarine warfare, and target towing. In all, the Grumman plant at Long Island, New York produced approximately 345 Gooses. On V-J Day, the US Navy canceled an order for 10 more.

After the Goose, Leroy Grumman continued to produce outstanding aircraft designs. Just before the attack on Pearl Harbor Roy had an idea for increasing the number of aircraft that could be loaded onto aircraft carriers. In demonstrating his design for the military, he used two paper clips stuck into either side of a rubber eraser to present a visual display of his folding wing design called the "Sto-Wing." During World War II, the "Grumman Iron Works" was the leading producer of aircraft, and therefore the leading supplier to the US Navy for fighter aircraft. The F4F Wildcat, F6F Hellcat, and the

TBF Avenger were all famous and effective products rolled out by the "Iron Works" that helped the Allies win the war.

At the end of the war, many Gooses were surplused by the military and these aircraft began to be put to work in civilian uses. Their ability to perform multiple roles in the most difficult conditions endeared the Goose to operators around the world. A quick look at the geographic distribution of the sturdy and multipurpose amphibian tells the story. Gooses were put to use in Alaska and the Aleutian Islands, Canada, the Caribbean, Florida, the Gulf of Mexico, South America, and the South Seas. Many may remember the 1970's TV series *Tales of the Gold Monkey* which revolved around the hero "Jake Cutter" and "Cutter's Goose." The many adventures encountered by "Jake" and his Goose are fairly representative of real life. Charter companies, scheduled airlines, Fish and Wildlife agencies, oil exploration companies, and a multitude of others utilized the Goose with its tremendous capabilities. Only about 50 Gooses are flying today. Other than possibly the Douglas DC-3, the Grumman Goose stands alone as a classic aircraft that strides proudly across generations. The Goose was one tough, talented, multipurpose aircraft, and it required men with the same attributes to fly these ships.

THE windows and windshields of this new Grumman G-21 amphibian are made of Plexiglas. This colorless transparent acrylic plastic is finding wide usage in all types of aircraft, both commercial and military, due to its light weight, ease of forming, and resistance against aging and weathering.

The latest in technology was used in the Grumman Goose when it was first produced in 1937. Over the next eight years, almost 350 of the G-21's were produced, serving many civilian and military aviation roles.

As an example, Goose number 45 (cactus-proof tires) was used for oil exploration in South America, passenger service to Catalina Island, and is now on display at the National Air and Space Museum in Washington, DC. About 50 of these rugged and remarkable amphibians are still being used today.

The Last Winged Sikorsky

"The work of the individual still remains the spark that moves mankind ahead"

- Igor Sikorsky 1889-1972

Igor Sikorsky was born in Russia in 1889. He was supremely interested in flight from his earliest days, but his main interest was in the helicopter. His early attempts at helicopter design were met with failure. He soon realized that the state of aerodynamic knowledge and engine design at that time were not yet ready for the challenge — so he switched to designing fixed wing aircraft. At the age of 21 he constructed in rapid succession two biplane aircraft, appropriately named the Sikorsky S-1 and S-2. They had 15 and 25 horsepower engines respectively. In 1911, he completed the S-4 and S-5, and received his airplane pilot's license from the Federation Aeornautique Internationale (only the 64th pilot in the world to do so). By 1913, he had designed and flown a four engine aircraft with a cabin *"luxuriously decorated, has four seats, a small sofa, and a table... In the rear was a wash room and a cabinet for clothing."*

Igor was the first person in history to pilot a four engine flying ship. To reward this feat, the Russian Emperor Czar Nicholas II gave him a gold watch. By early 1915, his four engine design had been pressed into service as a bomber against the Germans. When the Russian Communist Revolution intervened during the war, Igor was quick to leave his homeland. He said *"a profound demoralization was spreading like an epidemic of some new type of insanity."* Immediately after World War I, he took a steamer to New York because *"the United States seemed to me the only place which offered a real opportunity in what was then a rather precarious profession. Military aviation, and the industry that produced military aircraft, were completely in demobilization while private aviation was not born yet."* His passport simply stated his reason for wanting to enter the United States *"construct aircraft."*

For the next six years, Sikorsky continued to construct and improve his aircraft until May 21, 1927, a most famous date in aviation history. This is when the young Charles Lindbergh crossed the Atlantic - solo. This single event injected tremendous energy and inspiration into the public, the press, and the aviation industry. The very next year, Igor introduced his model S-38 to the world. It was a 10-seat amphibian with excellent range and capabilities. Pan Am, other airlines, the US Navy, and private individuals all purchased S-38's. In 1929, Lindbergh, on his 27th birthday, used a Pan Am S-38 to inaugurate the first foreign air mail service from Florida to the Panama Canal and Central-South America. Because of the wires, struts, and braces used in the design of the S-38, Lindbergh referred to S-38's as *"a collection of spare parts - flying in formation."* Also, in that same year, Western Air Express included a Sikorsky S-38 in its fleet providing passenger service between Wilmington, California and Catalina Island. In addition to Pan Am and WAE, NYRBA (New York-Rio-Buenos Aires Line, Inc.), and many other airlines put the S-38 to use in locations such as Hawaii and Canada.

The Sikorsky S-38 was at the forefront of long distance air travel in the early 1930's. The husband and wife team of intrepid motion picture photographer/explorers Martin and Osa Johnson used two different Sikorsky designs to unveil the beauty and mystery of the African Continent and other exotic locales to millions of moviegoers. They used a twin-engine S-38, painted with zebra stripes, named *Osa's Ark*, and a single-engine, S-39, painted with giraffe spots named *Spirit of Africa*. Martin had been bitten by the explorer bug when he worked as a cook for Jack London during the travels of the adventure writer. Another S-38 was used in the mid-1930's by the Johnson Wax Company (not related to Martin and Osa). Johnson's Wax purchased an S-38 to facilitate explorations and operations in Brazil—the only place where the Carnauba palm tree grew. The wax from this tree was and still is an important ingredient in many products. The Johnson Sikorsky was appropriately named *The Spirit of Carnauba*. A beautiful replica of this ship was built for Johnson Wax by the Born Again Res-

FROM COAST to COAST
IN A
SIKORSKY AMPHIBION

THE first transcontinental flight of a commercial amphibion has just been made from Curtiss Field, New York, to Los Angeles—and, of course, by a SIKORSKY AMPHIBION. Major C. C. Moseley, Operations Manager of the Western Air Express, Inc., who made the flight, accompanied by Arthur Goebel, of Hawaiian flight fame, is enthusiastic over the plane's performance, as his telegram shows.

GUARANTEES This wonderful craft, which is equally at home on the land, on the water and in the air, is *guaranteed*— to have a high speed of over 125 M.P.H., to have a ceiling of over 20,000 feet, and to fly—and climb—*on one motor* with pilot, mechanic, nine passengers and gasoline for a five hour flight.

Illustrated literature upon request

CURTISS FLYING SERVICE
INCORPORATED
GARDEN CITY — NEW YORK
SOLE SALES AGENT IN THE UNITED STATES

Manufactured by the SIKORSKY AVIATION CORPORATION, *College Point, L. I., N. Y.*

Igor Sikorsky named his new air yacht the "Amphibion" to set it apart from other designs. By the late 1920's his S-38 model was in service in the United States, the Territory of Hawaii, Central and South America, and in Asia. The pictured aircraft has "Los Angeles-To-Catalina Island" painted on the bow.

The Sikorsky S-38 established many firsts in the late 1920's and early 1930's. This advertisement touted Stanavo Oil for its use in an S-38 when it established three altitude records and one for speed in 1930. The chief test pilot for Sikorsky was Boris Sergievsky, who flew the ship when the records were set.

Part II — Water Striders

Colonel Charles A. Lindbergh—less than two years after his world record New York to Paris flight—flew a Sikorsky S-38 for Pan American Airways from Florida to the Panama Canal. This new air mail service flight was flown in Lindbergh's "giant twin-motored Sikorsky amphibian," stated the newspaper article.

On March 31, 1931, Pan Am with its amphibian aircraft created much good will in Central America and around the world. The airline was the immediate and continuing source of outside aid following the devastating Managua, Nicaragua earthquake.

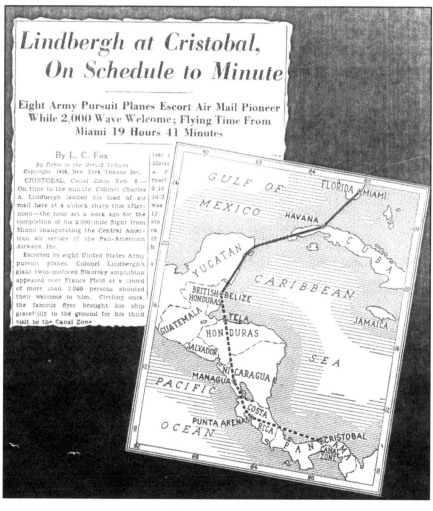

This beautiful Sikorsky S-39 reconstruction took 40 years to complete. Owners Dick and Pat Jackson of Rochester, New Hampshire tracked down the remains of this 1931 Sikorsky in Alaska in 1964. They gradually accumulated other parts from five different wrecked S-39's and then hand made the thousands of additional parts needed to complete the craft.

During the reconstruction, the Jacksons paid careful attention to every authentic detail. Items such as the white light at the top of the rudder used when the ship was running at harbor anchor and the life preserver on the wooden bulkhead door complete this magnificent project.

The Jacksons first flew their ship on the 4th of July, 2003 from their home field in New Hampshire. Later in the same month, the Jacksons flew the ship to the Experimental Aircraft Association annual fly-in at Oshkosh, Wisconsin where this photograph was taken. There, their magnificent reconstruction project won the prize for Antique Reserve Grand Champion. This ship is the oldest remaining flying Sikorsky in the world.

When asked how it felt to own a beautiful craft such as this one, Dick (wearing the pith helmet in the photo above) stated "We don't own antique aircraft... we are only temporary custodians: we just keep them a while before releasing them into the custody of the next generation."

This Sikorsky S-38 reconstruction shown here at the 2003 EAA fly-in is owned by Tom Schrade of Las Vegas, Nevada. It is painted like the ship that Martin Johnson flew in Africa in the 1930's. The interior is finished to resemble a luxurious yacht with beautiful mahogany paneling and a mini-bar for the passengers.

Captain Waldo Anderson in the cockpit of the Sikorsky S-38 during the 2003 EAA fly-in at Oshkosh, Wisconsin. The fly-in celebrated the 100th anniversary of the Wright brothers' first flight.

Oshkosh passengers enjoy the luxurious surroundings in Tom Shrade's S-38.

Passenger view of Oshkosh's Lake Winnebago while taxiing into position for takeoff.

A view of the S-38 and its own shadow over Lake Winnebago during the 2003 EAA annual fly-in at Oshkosh, Wisconsin.

storations company, who has also constructed a replica of the Martin and Osa Johnson zebra-striped S-38 *Osa's Ark*. The *Ark* is a beautiful ship now owned by Mr. Tom Schrade of Unlimited Adventures of Las Vegas. Both *Osa's Ark*, and a single-engine S-39, painted with giraffe spots and now named *Spirit of Igor* appeared at the Experimental Aircraft Association annual fly-in during the summer of 2003. These two ships flew together in front of thousands of attendees - it was the first time that these two craft had flown together in 70 years.

Pam Am's success with the S-38 led to bigger and better things for both the airline and for Sikorsky. With passenger and mail traffic to Central and South America growing rapidly, Sikorsky Aircraft was chosen to create a larger, more luxurious flying boat. In 1931, the S-40 *"Flying Clipper,"* as Sikorsky called it, began operations. This flying boat, originally designed as an amphibian, was the forerunner that established American airline operations as an international force. Only three of the S-40's were built and they were used exclusively by Pan Am Airways for their Trans-Caribbean routes.

This four-engine seaplane carried up to 45 passengers in walnut-paneled luxury and cruised at 110 MPH. In spite of the major advances the S-40 represented, it was not enough. Charles Lindbergh referred to this ship as the "flying forest" because of the strut and wire configuration of the craft. Even during the maiden flight, which was piloted by Lindbergh for Pan Am, discussions were held over dinner with fellow passengers Igor Sikorsky and Juan Trippe. They centered on creating a bigger, more efficient, and more refined flying boat for the next step — transoceanic flying — with sufficient capabilities to cross the oceans. Following these talks, one of the most handsome flying boats debuted in 1934. It was the Sikorsky S-42. The design was so successful that during a test flight in August test pilot Captains Lindbergh and Boris Sergievsky set no less than eight world records for aircraft performance in a single day.

A major media event occurred for the S-42 when on April 17, 1935 the *Pan American Clipper* departed on a survey flight with mail from Alameda, California, bound for Honolulu, Midway, Wake Island, and Guam. Thousands of spectators lined the water's edge to watch this adventurous departure. The pilot was the Pan Am veteran Edwin Musick and the navigator was Fred Noonan. On a sad note, Noonan disappeared with Amelia Earhart two years later on her attempt to cross the Pacific in her Lockheed Electra. On November 22, 1935, the US Postmaster General used Pan Am to inaugurate air mail service from the US to the Philippines and China. This time however, the flying boat that Pan Am used was the Martin M-130. Flights providing regular passenger service across the Pacific began in October 1936.

At left is one of three Sikorsky S-40 "Flying Clipper" ships that were built in 1931. They served the Central and South America routes for Pan Am. At right, sits a single-engine Sikorsky S-39. Notice the similar twin-tail boom, strut and wire construction for these "sister" ships.

The next year, these courageous exploits were portrayed in a classic movie entitled *China Clipper*. Starring Pat O'Brien, Humphrey Bogart, and Errol Flynn, it has wonderful footage of the Martin M-130. By July of 1937, in addition to the M-130, Sikorsky S-42 Clippers were also flying the Pacific, and they were in service across the Atlantic as well. On the Atlantic run, a circular route was followed from the United States to England, through Portugal, the Azores, Bermuda, and finally back to the United States.

By the mid 1930's, Pan Am owner, Juan Trippe had switched to Boeing as his supplier of seaplanes. Sikorsky, with the domestic passenger market for his seaplanes now out of his reach, secured a contract from the US Navy to build a huge flying boat "The Flying

Dreadnought." While the design was impressive, the costs were too high for the Navy to order more than the one prototype that was built. This successful design however, attracted the attention of a Pan Am competitor - American Export Airlines (AEA). In December 1939, AEA contracted with Sikorsky, now under the name Vought-Sikorsky, to construct the VS-44A flying boat. AEA already owned a fleet of oceangoing ships named *Excalibur, Exeter*, and *Excambian* and they decided to give their three new flying boats the same names.

Designed to fly nonstop across the Atlantic, this new flying boat was faster and had greater range than any prior models. The model VS-44A was the last fixed wing aircraft that Igor ever built. As soon as his design work was completed on this last seaplane, he began to work on his long sought after goal of creating the helicopter. In less that 30 years, beginning in his backyard with a ship made from sticks, wires and turnbuckles, Igor Sikorsky had contributed to air travel on an international scale. As Igor states in his book, The Winged S, *"Indeed, the progress of aviation... was remarkable during this short period of one generation."*

Charles Blair

There are two men who played significant roles in the flying life of the VS-44A's: Charles (Charlie) F. Blair and Wilton (Dick) R. Probert. Charlie Blair first soloed in 1928 at the age of 19. After acquiring his Navy wings at Pensacola Naval Air Station, he flew for the Navy, and later became a pilot for Boeing Air Transport (now United Air Lines). By 1940, he was the Chief Pilot for American Export Airlines. Working for AEA, Blair was the original test pilot for all three VS-44As, and he also flew them regularly across the Atlantic, throughout the war. Beginning in 1942, while flying as an AEA employee for the Naval Air Transport Service (NATS), Charlie set many records flying nonstop across the Atlantic in the VS-44s. Although these were dangerous missions, he clearly enjoyed flying the big Sikorskys when he said *"My feeling for this big seaplane...had by now become affectionate and possessive."*

All throughout World War II, NATS used these big boats to carry Navy brass, USO performers, and government representatives to and from Europe, Africa, and South America. Passenger lists included such notables as General Omar Bradley, Humphrey Bogart, Edward G. Robinson, Douglas Fairbanks, Jr., Eleanor Roosevelt, and Queen Wilhelmina of the Netherlands. The Queen was living in exile in England during the occupation of her home country, but she flew to visit her children who were living in Canada at the time. Carrying passengers of such notoriety, it should be mentioned that these AEA ships were the first in the history of the world to employ stewardesses on transatlantic passenger flights. Some of these flights lasted for 24 hours or more which prompted some of the AEA stewardesses to joke that they had "walked to Europe."

Of the three VS-44A's, two were lost in crashes, both because of pilot error. *Excalibur* was lost in October 1942 during a takeoff in Newfoundland. *Exeter* crashed in 1947 during a night landing near Montevideo, Uruguay, near where the German battle cruiser *Graf Spee* lay on the bottom following her wartime sinking. *Exeter* had been hauling guns to the rebels there. After the war ended, the only remaining Sikorsky flying boat, air registration # N41881 or simply "881" for short, was briefly used in a commercial venture in 1947 by Charles Blair for charter flying. During succeeding years, other charter owners tried various schemes, with little success. In the 1950's, 881 wound up on a beach in Ancon, a small town on the coast of Peru about 30 miles north of Lima. The previous charter owner had gotten into financial trouble and 881 had been sitting on the beach for about 18 months. From the beach, she was rescued by the second important figure in the flying life of 881, Dick Probert.

Although Dick Probert will be discussed in greater detail later in this book, it is important to recognize what an important part he played in the future of this last winged Sikorsky. I don't know why they haven't made a movie about his amazing story. Perhaps it is because, even with all of Hollywood's ability to manufacture hot stars and create special digital effects, it is not possible to duplicate the men and machines involved. I will greatly simplify this real life adventure.

Dick Probert owned Avalon Air Transport in Long Beach, California which flew to Avalon Bay. He had been using Grumman Gooses on this route since 1953 and when he heard about the flying boat in 1957, he figured that it could carry many times the amount of passengers that a Goose could. This looked like a money making proposition.

Dick flew to Lima with cash and a mechanic. The Flight Engineer for the prior owners, who still lived in Lima, had not been paid, and he had retained part of the beaching gear so that the plane could not be removed before he was paid the money due. Dick made two trips to Lima to get the big Sikorsky. He encountered various problems with the flying boat—magnetos, gasoline, a wing float broken on takeoff, and with the Mexican authorities while en route to the United States. Finally, he was able to fly 881 back to Long Beach.

Dick Probert had many adventures getting his newly purchased Sikorsky VS-44A ready to fly from South America to Long Beach, California. This photograph, taken in Peru, shows the temporary dock setup to allow work to be performed on the magnetos. The name Excalibur was not the one she was born with. Excambian was her name at launch in early 1942.

The story of the magneto problem is worth examining in more detail. Confronted with more than 1,200 miles of open ocean flying to get his newly acquired ship from Peru to California, Probert had decided to use celestial navigation—which is best done at night. His takeoff from Ancon was planned for just after sunset to take advantage of the night skies aloft. The takeoff went smoothly, but after about ten minutes, almost simultaneously, the magnetos in two of the four engines malfunctioned, forcing Dick to look for a place to set the big ship down. The odds were stacked against him. He was going to attempt a landing at night, in an unfamiliar ship that was overloaded with gasoline and spare parts. In addition, he was about to land in an unlit harbor, under a low overcast.

When describing this particular adventure, Probert stated that this was the scariest situation that he had ever been in (concerning aircraft, that is). *"It was a time when I should have been scared, but don't remember being scared"* he said. For this emergency landing he had *"strangers for a crew, only two take offs and landings in the ship, it was night time with no moon, no lights were required on boats in the harbor, the maximum fuel load was 3,800 gallons - but we had 4,200 gallons on board, so we tried a landing outside the harbor. I flew over the town at night with a low propeller pitch setting—to create the maximum amount of noise to attract attention—and then I set controls for steady descent at 200' per minute and then waited for something to happen."* He said *"During the ten years that I flew the Sikorsky, that was the best landing I ever had."* Despite the odds, Probert landed safely that night.

After many attempts to diagnose and remedy the magneto troubles, the ship was finally ready for the long flight up the coast of South America, Central America, Mexico, and on to her new home in Long Beach, California. During the hairy final take-off for home, the starboard pontoon caught on the water and broke exactly in half—lodging in the wing. Figuring that the repair facilities in Ancon, Peru were probably less than what was required, Dick continued on toward Mexico. After flying all night, they landed at 9:30 a.m. in Acapulco. After many adventures with the Mexican authorities, repairs were made and permission was granted for departure.

Dick and his crew then successfully made it back to Long Beach with 881 (with about 15 minutes of gas left in the tanks). He flew 881 on a regular schedule carrying up to 47 passengers—every summer for the next ten years—between Long Beach Harbor and Avalon Bay, without incident. At the end of that time—because FAA regulations required that pilots flying for scheduled airlines be under the age of 60—Probert was forced to retire from flying the Sikorsky in 1967. He then decided to sell 881 to—where else—the first pilot that had flown her, Charles Blair.

To return to Charlie's story, after World War II, he joined the Air Force where he proceeded to set more major flying records, particularly in the area of polar route navigation. By the early 1960's, he had formed an airline of his own in the Virgin Islands, which he named Antilles Air Boats. Dick Probert felt that Charlie Blair and his airline would be the perfect owner and the perfect use for 881. With the purchase and addition of the big Sikorsky to the existing fleet of Grumman Gooses, Antilles Air Boats soon became the largest amphibian airline in the world. In 1968, continuing his impossible list of accomplishments, Charles Blair married actress Maureen O'Hara. She promptly also fell in love with 881. Antilles Air Boats continued its prosperity but, in 1978, Charles Blair was killed in the crash of an AAB

After snagging the right pontoon during takeoff from Ancon, Peru, Captain Probert flew the ship in that condition until repairs could be made in Acapulco, Mexico.

Part II — Water Striders

Captain Dick Probert takes off from Avalon Bay in the mid-1960's with a few dock boys as passengers. This photo was taken for a publicity shot by long-time photography store owner - Gene Smith of Gene's Photo Shop in Avalon. Gene was a large man who was not used to small boats. For this shot, he was put under great pressure to get it right the first time.

Captain Probert did not want to make another take off and Gene did not want to be in the ocean in a small wooden skiff any longer than required. The author and fellow dock boy Rodney Zane Wilcox held on to the back of Gene's belt to steady him for the one take opportunity. Gene did an excellent job framing the flying boat between the Casino and, on the hill, the Zane Grey Pueblo and the Chimes Tower. Rodney Wilcox lived just down the street from the Pueblo and his middle name was inspired by the proximity to Zane Grey's former home.

The Sikorsky flew between Long Beach Harbor and Avalon Bay from 1957 to 1967 carrying thousands of happy travelers to and from the "Island of Romance."

Goose. Because of his fantastic career, exploits, and contributions to his country, Brigadier General Charles F. Blair is now buried in Arlington National Cemetery across the Potomac from Washington, DC.

During the flying life of N41881, she had possessed many nicknames: Excambian, Flying Ace, Mother Goose, Super Goose, and Queen of the Sky. Maureen O'Hara has stated that Charlie used to refer to 881 as the "Queen of the Sky," and that he referred to Maureen as the "Queen of the Earth." In return, she referred to him as "King of the Earth," and she called 881 "Charlie's Queen." After Charlie's death, Maureen continued to own and manage Antilles Air Boats, filling the role of the only woman in the world to own an airline.

After the Sikorsky VS-44A flying boat was retired by Antilles Air Boats in the late1970's, 881 was donated to the Naval Air Museum in Pensacola, Florida. From there, she was transferred to the New England Air Museum where she underwent a complete restoration — a prodigious feat which took more than 10 years to complete. This major project involved a team of over one hundred volunteers, including several of the original Sikorsky employees who had built her in 1942. N41881 is the last of the American-built flying boats still in existence. When the restoration project was completed, with Dick Probert and his wife Nancy (Ince) Probert in attendance, Maureen O'Hara dedicated the beautifully restored *Excambian* to the New England Air Museum at Windsor Locks, Connecticut in the summer of 1997.

Thus, with the last of the big flying boats removed from the rolls of active airliners, was ended one of the most important, romantic, and historic eras in commercial aviation. Both the Atlantic and the Pacific Oceans had been conquered by Sikorsky, Martin, and Boeing flying boats. At the beginning of this very short period in history, the world appeared large and challenging. By the end of this Golden Age the world had become much smaller. Airline travel was rapidly changing from an exciting adventure to simply a part of modern life. It was all over. Less than two dozen big seaplanes, stately flying ocean liners, had zoomed onto the world stage, only to be overshadowed by land-based planes in less than ten years. And then, they quietly slipped from view. Time had left them in its wake.

> *"The conquest of the air, with its profoundly important influence on the history of humanity will remain one of the outstanding facts of the twentieth century."*
>
> - Igor Sikorsky

Part II — Water Striders

During the formative years of commercial air travel, amphibians and flying boats were extremely successful. The only remaining American-made flying boat, of all those produced, is the VS-44A which is now on permanent display at the New England Air Museum in Connecticut - near where she first flew in 1942.

Manufacturer	Model	Production Began	Number Built	Number Remaining
Twin-engine Amphibians				
Sikorsky	*S-38*	1928	111	2
Douglas	*Dolphin*	1931	58	1
Grumman	*Goose*	1937	345	50
Four-engine Flying Boats				
Sikorsky	*S-40*	1931	3	0
Sikorsky	*S-42*	1934	10	0
Martin	*M-130*	1935	3	0
Boeing	*B-314*	1939	12	0
Sikorsky	*VS-44*	1942	3	1

PART III — The Knights of Avalon

"Checking out pilots in land planes is never so much of a problem. But flying boats are different. For every take off and landing, the pilot must build his own airport out of a new combination of winds and waves. Even the chore of tying up to a mooring can be a frustrating task."

- Charles Blair in "The Red Ball In The Sky"

The term "intrepid pioneers" does not seem to have enough letters in it to describe those pilots who blazed trails into the skies and around the world. As far as we know, we only live once and, therefore, we only get to know those people who accompany us during our short stay here on earth. Having the opportunity to know the pilots—and others—on the following pages, adds tremendous knowledge, enjoyment, and spice to the lives of all who take this trip.

Dick Probert

Captain Probert struggled to control his Vengeance dive bomber as he dove at a steep angle directly toward the Cumberland River. The flight controls had locked during the flight testing of this new ship and he was rapidly heading straight for disaster. He quickly deployed the dive brakes to slow the descent and regain control of his ship. During World War II he had been hired as a personal pilot to one of the executives of Consolidated-Vultee Aircraft Company of Nashville, Tennessee. This particular Consolidated facility produced the Vengeance dive-bomber, a large single-engine ship created to counter the German Stuka dive-bomber. The huge aircraft assembly plant at Nashville employed thousands of people and ran 24 hours a day.

Another exciting incident occurred involving Dick Probert over Nashville. One day in September 1942 a patriotic rally/war bond drive was scheduled at the war plant. The rally starred Hollywood actor Andy Devine, actress Laraine Day, and World War I medal winner Sergeant Alvin York. They were to appear in front of the combined shifts at the factory. Someone thought that it would be a good idea to have an airshow as a warm up so Dick Probert jumped into one of the new bombers. During the demonstration, a part of the engine ducting broke off and came out the top of the cowling. Three actions immediately followed; Dick brought the ship in for repairs, the airshow was ended, and neither Andy, Laraine, nor Alvin accepted the offer of a free airplane ride. Dick's work for Consolidated was only one small part of his career in aviation that has spanned almost 100 years.

Part III — The Knights of Avalon

Dick was born Wilton R. Probert on Valentine's Day 1907 in Ohio. He attended Holmes High School in Covington, Kentucky and later, after he and his parents moved out west, they landed in Hollywood, California. Dick's father set up a sheet metal shop in Los Angeles. Dick, who had just graduated from high school, drove the Model-T Ford delivery truck for the Larson Auto Parts supply store. He attacked the driving job with vigor and rapidly advanced at the store. In addition to possessing an innate sense of urgency, he had good handwriting which allowed him to quickly progress to the front counter, answering the phone, and then taking customer orders. Within a few years, he had succeeded as the auto supply store manager.

All through his life Dick has been passionate about aviation. As a teenager, he had seen many exciting aviation events. The introduction of observation and combat aircraft during World War I, the barnstorming pilots of the 1920's, the Academy Award winning movie *Wings*—which he saw several times upon its release—and Lindbergh's Transatlantic solo flight all combined to fire his imagination. By the age of 22, Dick was taking flying lessons and, after 9 hours and 45 minutes of accumulated solo flying time, he passed his flight test for a private pilot's license. Dick explains that in those days, the exam consisted of *"a figure eight over the airport—shut the engine off and land back at the same airport."* As the young, single store manager, Dick soon earned enough cash to enroll in the Curtiss-Wright Technical Institute and then to purchase his own airplane - an OX-5 Command Aire. This was an open cockpit bi-plane with two seats—the pilot usually sat in the back and the passenger in the front.

Now that he owned an airplane, Dick left the auto parts business and opened his own flying school—Probert School of Aeronautics. In addition—with typical exuberance—he explored southern California, took friends up for rides, trained students, and flew semi-official charters. On one flight, Patrick Knowles was a passenger with Dick. Patrick was a movie star with Warner Bros. Studios, where he often co-starred with Errol Flynn. Patrick decided to fly to Santa Barbara for a visit. The newspaper headline from February 21, 1932 read as follows:

QUEER DISEASE GRIPS PLANES

"Carburetor Cancer" or "Falling Sickness" Always Seems to Strike Them Over Santa Barbara and They Have to Make "Forced Landing" Despite Ban

2/21/32

SANTA BARBARA, Feb. 22.—An airplane owned by W. R. Probert, Los Angeles flyer, is the latest to fall victim to the mysterious ailment of "carburetor cancer" affecting all planes which land on the Casa Loma airport, which lies within the city limits.

Following protests several weeks ago, the City Council passed an ordinance prohibiting the use of the field as an airport. The Councilmen, in the ordinance, however, made no provision for forced landings.

And now, it seems, every plane which lands on the field develops "Carburetor Cancer" as soon as local police, summoned by irate neighbors, reach the field and start an investigation. The disease, the flyers tell police, invariably causes forced landings.

And as in the case of other planes, the Probert plane, on taking off from the field after its "forced landing" recovered immediately.

So police, balked in their efforts to combat the dread disease, are finding it rather difficult to enforce the ordinance effectively.

Dick always seemed to be testing the limits of this new world of aviation. At his father's sheet metal shop, he had his dad make an insert for the Command Aire's front passenger seat that allowed space for a second passenger. Two friends of Dick's in the auto parts trade

Teenage "hanger helper" and future pilot Warren Stoner with Dick Probert in front of his J-5 Travel Air at the Probert School of Aeronautics at Van Nuys airport in southern California.

heard about the airplane and decided that they would love to fly past Catalina Island to San Clemente Island to go bird hunting. On one cool fall morning, all three climbed into the modified ship loaded down with their hunting gear and their heavy clothes for the 50 mile open cockpit flight across the blue Pacific. Dick figured that he could fly to and from the island and be back in time for his afternoon session with a student pilot. During takeoff, Dick noticed that he took more runway than usual before lifting off but he still had some distance to go before the end of runway. They landed on the island and the hunting went well.

The departure was a different story. The afternoon had heated up by the time the hunters returned with a couple of bags of birds. Because planes don't fly as well in warmer temperatures, Probert had taken the precaution of placing a marker along side the grass strip at the last point of safe departure. Because he was in his mid-20's Dick's attitude was *"if you can get it in the plane, I can fly it."* The plane took too long to lift off and the ship skidded and flipped on its back injuring all three. The island's resident sheepherder couldn't help transport them because his wife had taken the only boat on the island to the mainland. Back at the airport in the LA Valley, the student pilot who was scheduled for a training flight was concerned that Probert and his plane were not there so he began making phone calls. Finally, a Wrigley Douglas Dolphin flew over the island, spotted the wreckage, and called the Coast Guard who sent a rescue boat. Probert said *"and that was the end of my OX-5 Command Aire."*

Probert School of Aeronautics (PSA) was located at the Van Nuys, California airport. One particular student that Probert taught to fly was a barber who worked at the Lakeside Golf Club in Studio City. The barber was quite pleased with Dick as his instructor and he referred many of his own barbershop clients to PSA. As you can imagine, the clients of a golf course barbershop located in the middle of Studio City are generally actors. The result was that Probert trained several popular actors of the 1930's including Roscoe Ates, Barton McClain, Dick Purcell, and Richard Arlen.

Richard Arlen was one of the stars in the Academy Award winning movie *Wings*, and he was also the owner of the Lakeside Golf Club. He asked Dick to fly over and land in his rather large back yard to pick him up for his first lesson. Probert landed in the back yard without difficulty but the take off was another story. The yard dimensions only allowed for a short take off run and the surrounding trees only increased the challenge. In order to take off, Dick had to roll his plane onto one side and fly between the trees vertically. Dick remembers telling Arlen *"you realize that this is a makeshift deal"* and from then on, they used the Van Nuys airport as their point of departure. During one lesson, Arlen asked Dick to land on his golf course. They landed, taxied right up to the club house, whereupon the manager came racing out to the plane to complain. When the manager saw that the passenger was the owner of the club, all he could do was turn and walk away.

Dick Probert felt that Richard Arlen had been so positively impressed by his flight training experience at PSA that he got up his courage to ask the powerful Hollywood star if he would be interested in investing in a flight school. To Dick's surprise, Arlen accepted and PSA was immediately replaced by Arlen-Probert Aviation. As business boomed, one of the new students that Dick trained at Arlen-Probert was Hollywood actor Andy Devine—who would figure prominently in Dick's future. Andy was a very memorable character actor with a high-pitched voice that was the result of a childhood accident. He was in the 1939 movie *Stagecoach* with John Wayne and later, he was sidekick to Roy Rogers and other cowboy stars. Dick Probert had soloed Andy on December 2, 1941. Andy made one solo flight around the Newhall airport, but it was the last flight he could make for several years—war clouds were looming on the immediate horizon.

The attack on Pearl Harbor in 1941 brought about drastic changes in every facet of life, Arlen-Probert Aviation included. Civilian aircraft were kept under strict control and limited to airport pattern flying only. This continued for a short time until, as Probert said, *"some fool flew over Los Angeles at night."* Army Air Force fighters were scrambled, the press added to the uproar, and panic was widespread. This brought civilian flying to a complete halt. Unable to make a living at flight training, Probert temporarily took a job with TWA in Albuquerque, New Mexico teaching military pilots to fly B-24 heavy bombers. Dick worked one short job after another; serving as an airline inspector for the Civil Aeronautic Association (Dick didn't like it), and then as a pilot for Consolidated-Vultee Vengeance dive-bomber plant in Tennessee.

Consolidated-Vultee Aircraft Company had a separate division named Consairways which contracted with the military to transport personnel and supplies throughout the Pacific war theater of operations. Looking for a change, Dick got an assignment with Consairways. The War Manpower Commission selected him to become an Aviation Pilot Officer and Flight Captain for the Army Air Transport Command (ATC) based in San Francisco, California. From there, Dick flew converted B-24 Liberator bombers (once modified for

Captain Dick Probert in front of his modified Liberator bomber (C-87) in Manila, Philippines in 1944. The other crew members are navigator Don Dudlext, co-pilot Orr, and radio operator Phil Callahan.

transport they were referred to as C-87's) to points all over the South Pacific war zone. Brisbane, Canton Island, Johnston Island, Tarawa, Guadalcanal, New Caledonia, Hawaii, and the Philippines were all ports of call. Some of the Consairways C-87's were converted to carry up to 27 passengers, some of which were *"plushed up"* with upholstered seats according to Dick. These ships were used to transport military brass between operations centers—usually San Francisco and Australia.

Two particular trips across the Pacific during the war stand out in Dick's memory. During one, Dick was the Captain of a Consairways C-87 that was flying from American Samoa to Hawaii when he received a radio distress call from a C-47 pilot who was ditching in the Pacific because of mechanical problems. Dick searched for the troubled ship and located it just before it ditched in the rough seas. Captain Probert radioed the position of the four survivors who were now climbing into a life raft. As Dick continued to circle, the Navy immediately dispatched a PBY Catalina amphibian to the scene for rescue. The PBY arrived, picked up the downed crew, and attempted to take off in the stormy seas. During the take off, the PBY hit a huge wave and one of its propellers flew off, killing the pilot. Continuing to circle, Probert once again radioed for assistance. His own ship was now running low on fuel and he could remain on station for only a short time. He radioed the base and this time he asked the Navy to dispatch a surface ship to rescue the flyers, and also to send a replacement for his aircraft to keep watch on the survivors' location. Finally, an Army C-47 arrived and Captain Probert returned to Samoa to refuel.

A second trip was memorable thanks to a combination of unique weather phenomena. During this trip Dick set a speed record from Hawaii to the mainland which stood for 5 years. The flight was between Honolulu, Hawaii and Travis Air Force base located near Sacramento, California. At the time, there was a low pressure system over Hawaii and a high pressure system over the western US. The winds circulating around the two systems aloft combined to give him a tail wind for the entire trip which allowed him to cover the 2240 miles in 8:54 (normally a 13 hour flight).

Finally, after 42 round trips across the Pacific, Probert went back into private aviation when the war ended. He contacted his former student and friend Andy Devine and they formed the Probert-Devine

Dick Probert, Andy Devine, and his wife Dorothy prepare to depart from Whiteman Airpark for a vacation in Ensenada, Mexico in 1946. The dog got to go, too.

Aviation Corporation. Using two PT-26 aircraft, good instruction, and good management, they successfully took advantage of the pent up demand for flight training. One major ingredient toward their success was the financial support that the government provided through the post-war GI Bill to veterans who were aspiring flight students. However, after a few years Congress decided to end the GI Bill payments and the large reservoir of students dried up. Dick was again forced back into the job market and he took a position flying non-scheduled trips using Douglas DC-3's and DC-4's between Burbank, California, Chicago, and New York.

Avalon Air Transport

During the early 1950's, Dick's former student and friend Bob Hanley contacted Dick about a money making idea. Bob Hanley was working as a pilot flying for Macco Construction at the time, and he

Avalon Air Transport began operations in Avalon bay with one Grumman Goose in 1953. In later years, from five to seven Gooses were in service.

had been contacted by a group of Santa Catalina Island boosters who were exploring the feasability of an air taxi service which could supply steady passenger flying to Avalon Bay. Avalon, with its rich tradition of air travel, had been without amphibian air service for several years. Both Hanley and Probert took the steamer to Avalon where they talked with the city boosters and the City Mayor - Merle Porter. They were met with great enthusiasm by city government and the business community who welcomed the potential boost in trade and tourism.

Heartened by the positive reception from the city fathers, Dick knew that he would also need the acquiescence (if not the blessing) of the owner of the island, Philip Wrigley, in order for his new enterprise to succeed. Philip, you may recall, was a founder and a major player in United Air Lines which flew scheduled flights in DC-3's to the Airport in the Sky in the interior of the island. A quick check with UAL, Wrigley's Santa Catalina Island Company, and local boat operators revealed some trepidation but Dick began preparations for a seaplane base anyway. By early 1953, Dick had invested much of his

By the late 1950's, AAT operated 3 DC-3's in addition to the amphibian operations. From left are Captains' Probert, Bill Kilgour, Fred Pierce, and other pilots including Lloyd "Jugs" Burkhard (center - dark jacket), and George Briggs—co-pilot on the Sikorsky flying boat (second from right).

own savings and had taken on a financial partner, Jean Chisholm, to begin the new airline. They purchased one Grumman Goose from Cordova Airlines in Alaska and began putting the operation together. They named the new airline Avalon Air Transport and began operations on August 27, 1953 with one Goose, two pilots, and a small office staff. On the first day only six passengers were carried. But that number doubled every day for a week. Soon, there were over 100 fare paying passengers per day. Cost for the Goose flight at that time, from Long Beach airport to Avalon, was $6.58 round trip.

Initially, rather than flying direct to Avalon Bay, Probert used a T-shaped floating dock anchored in a semi-open sea position in Descanso Bay in front of the Hotel St. Catherine. Although Dick had received approval for his operations from almost everyone concerned, the Avalon Harbor Master felt that seaplane activities would conflict with the boat traffic in the bay that usually persisted until the Labor Day holiday. In addition to the Harbor Master, the Miss Catalina speedboats, the shore boats, and the glass bottomed boats (owned by the Wrigley's SCI Co.) formed a block in opposition to the fledgling airline. This opposition was all but eliminated because of an accident that occurred during a baseball game in Avalon.

The son of the Standard Oil distributor in Avalon — a grade school student — was hit in the eye during a game and severely injured. The only way to save the young man's life was to get advanced emergency treatment at a full service medical facility on the mainland. The problem was that all of the conventional transportation was unable to operate because of weather conditions. UAL could not fly to the Airport in the Sky because clouds obscured the runway, and there was a heavy storm at sea that prohibited boat travel. Faced with this dilemma, the SCI Co. contacted AAT for assistance. Probert agreed and immediately a Goose was flown across the storm ravaged channel, landed, and met the paramedics at the storm damaged floats. The injured young man was transported to the mainland where he was treated and later, fully recovered. By mid-September, Avalon Air had moved operations to the Pleasure Pier in the middle of Avalon Harbor.

After the prime summer travel season tourist travel to the island drops off, but AAT made it through the first winter with help from the United Air Lines counter personnel at Long Beach airport. They looked favorably upon the new airline and when the Airport in the Sky was fogged in, they sent passengers to Avalon Air Transport. The next summer was "a roaring success" as Probert added more Gooses and secured the contract to carry the US Mail to Avalon. As time went along, Probert's airline and reputation grew. Additional medical emergencies—such as making an open-sea, night landing to deliver Red Cross blood supplies to the island following a boat explosion— and other exploits contributed to the Probert persona. He had a reputation for tackling the most difficult situations. Whenever his pilots would return from the island without landing in the bay because of bad weather, Dick took it as a personal challenge to take the flight and land safely. Even the Avalon station personnel had a saying that the "skies would clear" or the "sea would smooth" when it heard that "DP" was flying. In spite of this display of skill and bravado, Dick Probert never asked any of his pilots to do anything that he would not do himself.

Momentum rapidly built toward the success of AAT. A solid reputation for performance and community service, the US Mail contract, and labor strikes affecting boat traffic all contributed. In 1954, because Dick needed a managing partner, Jean Chisolm's 50% of stock was purchased by Walt von Kleinsmid. Walt was tall, mild mannered, brilliant, and had a gift for running a business. His analytical abilities and business acumen were a wonderful counter-balance to the "full speed ahead" Probert approach. These two men, over time, built a very successful operation. In November 1958 a longshoreman strike left all boats serving the island tied up at their moorings. Filling in, AAT hauled an average of 6,000 pounds per day to the island on Gooses. The normal freight charge of 5 cents per pound was reduced by Dick Probert and Walt von Kleinsmid to 3 cents per pound for the duration of the strike. During the 15 years that they owned AAT, they employed hundreds of personnel. Pilots (water qualified), stewardesses, aircraft and engine mechanics, station personnel, and

Part III — The Knights of Avalon

Walt von Kleinsmid and Dick Probert at the Long Beach harbor seaplane base with a plaque of appreciation awarded to them by the citizens of Avalon.

dock boys all contributed. Aircraft, floats, boats, baggage carts, delivery vans, tools, parts, and uniforms all were purchased. Probert gradually added 2 Gooses from the Peruvian Air Force for $8,000 apiece, 6 Gooses from Mexico, and 3 DC-3's for flights where water landings were not necessary.

The development of the seaplane base in Avalon Bay took time, creative thought, and the assistance of several talented people before its final design was competed. One man in particular, Al Hanson and his work boat the *Can Do*, were primarily responsible for much of the placement and set up of the docks, lines, and cables that were used for both the summer and winter operations. It took much trial and error to finally achieve the best layout. Hanson especially had to rise to the challenge when Probert added the Sikorsky 47 passenger flying boat to the fleet in 1957. The first method for docking the Sikorsky, which

The author's son Greg in the appropriately named "Woody boat" along-side the seaplane floats in Avalon - October, 1967. A new breakwater is under construction in the background.

has no brakes or reverse, was by use of a winch and cable—a fairly hazardous operation. Ultimately, the layout and procedures were so streamlined that the big flying boat could make 10 or 12 trips a day in and out of the base without too much hazard to life, limb, or boats. The docks on the Long Beach harbor side were more protected and less congested—therefore only one boat was necessary for that operation. Two boats were used to dock the Sikorsky in Avalon—the "Woody" boat, and the "Tinny" boat. George Gemilere of Avalon built the "woody" boat which gave many years of great service. It was used in many ways: to attach the lines to the Sikorsky and, using its padded bow, to push the flying boat up to the floats, to deliver freight, to load and unload planes when they could not come to the docks, and—on occasion—to transport revelers and supplies to "after hours" beach parties down the coast.

In addition to the regularly scheduled flights from the mainland to the island, special charters and the US Navy contributed to the thriving airline. On one charter, Dick flew Charles Lindbergh and his party to Mulege, Baja California on a trip concerning the study of the ecology of birds and fish in the region. At one point, Dick asked his hero for an autograph. Dick had brought along a song sheet dated 1927—the year of Lindbergh's famous flight—but Charles had to decline because he felt that there would be problems with the sheet music publishers. Dick Probert with his Hollywood connections was also hired for the filming of movies and TV shows of the 1950's and 1960's. On the popular TV series *Seahunt* starring Lloyd Bridges, Dick, flying a Goose, was featured in several episodes. In a movie starring James Cagney entitled *The Gallant Hours*, Dick was seen flying the Sikorsky flying boat.

Another charter flight, returning from Mexico, ran out of fuel over the Pacific Ocean north of San Diego. The pilot, Captain Bill Kilgour, had to set the Goose down at sea near the US Navy facilities on San Clemente Island. Captain Kilgour was picked up and the Goose was sealed up for the night to drift at sea. In the morning, the Navy personnel on San Clemente helped with the towing and refueling for the trip home. Meanwhile, back at the Long Beach airport, co-owner

Three Gooses wait on their moorings during a lull in the flight schedule as the Sikorsky taxiis toward the dock in 1960. In later years, the Gooses were updated with 3-bladed propellers for added performance. Two of the Gooses were also modified with retractable wing floats so that they could carry eleven passengers rather than the normal payload of nine.

of the airline Walt von Kleinsmid saw the morning headlines in the newspaper which screamed "Catalina Plane Lost At Sea." Walt saw this paper in the vending machine at the airport terminal, inserted 25 cents and retrieved all of the papers from the machine before any potential passengers had a chance to read them. The owner of the gift shop in the terminal saw what Walt was doing, bought some papers before he could get there and made Walt pay full price for her remaining copies. The only damage to the Goose was a dented wing float—which attests to the excellent flying abilities of the pilot.

During Dick Probert's long and illustrious career in aviation, he logged over 35,000 flight hours in aircraft both large and small. He flew single and multi-engine craft in land and water operations—both in war and in peacetime. For the 10 years that Dick flew the Sikorsky he logged 7,260 round trips, not counting charters and movie appearances. In August of 1960 he flew 11 round trips in one day.

This man, this rugged individualist with the stern visage, who inspired awe (and sometimes fear in his employees) has been a major factor in many peoples lives. He is a legend. Even today, former employees recount that when Dick used the teletype to contact Avalon from the mainland over 25 miles away, you could hear spines crack in the Avalon office as everyone snapped to attention whenever the teletype clacked to life with the dreaded line *"This is DP."* In the 15 years that Dick Probert owned and operated Avalon Air Transport/Catalina Air Lines—the name was changed in 1964—the achievement that he is most proud of is his safety record while carrying over 200,000 passengers with the Sikorsky flying boat, DC-3's, and Grumman Gooses.

During interviews with Dick Probert some interesting points were revealed regarding the characteristics of good aircraft pilots—water pilots in particular. Good pilots use finesse and do not over control, he said. This is usually the product of experience—the ability to anticipate the correct action—before a more drastic maneuver is required. For water landings, a good pilot must be able to read the wind and water conditions—looking for any clue that he can find. Smoke, flags, boats, white caps, and patterns on the surface are many of the water indicators used. Many times, in rougher conditions, it might take 15 minutes waiting for the perfect wind and swell conditions for landing. It is usually recommended to land parallel to the swells which calls for a cross-wind landing—requiring excellent skills from the pilot.

When asked to compare the twin engine Goose with the four engine flying boat, Dick feels that the Goose was harder to fly because it took more concentration for successful takeoffs and landings—while the Sikorsky 881 flying boat was more fun. The last 881 flight for Catalina Air Lines was on a clear, sunny day in September of 1966. This final flyover of Avalon bay by Probert in the big Sikorsky was escorted by two Gooses in close formation. It was bitter-sweet to watch as the three ships climbed and turned into the sky away from the pier and out into the San Pedro channel.

Nancy Ince-Probert

Nancy looked eagerly over the cliff from the back of her horse as she watched the filming of the TV series in the sea cove below. She had ridden her horse through a neighbor's property in the exclusive Palos Verdes Peninsula area of Los Angeles. This area of Spanish style homes with swimming pools, tennis courts, horse stables, and white painted fences was the backdrop as she watched a production of an episode of *Seahunt* that was being filmed near the Marineland aquarium. But it wasn't the star of the series, Lloyd Bridges, that she had come to see... it was Dick Probert, whom she would eventually marry.

The film industry was second nature to Nancy. As mentioned earlier, Nancy's grandfather Thomas Harper Ince was a movie producer in New York before he moved to Hollywood and set up *Inceville* in 1911. Thomas had two brothers who were also in the film industry. John Ince was an actor for many years, and Ralph was an actor and director until his early death in a car crash while filming a movie in England. In addition to the film industry, Nancy's grandfather Thomas enjoyed horses, boats, and aviation. He owned a 98' schooner named "Edris," and an airport named Ince Field near Culver City, California. At one time, he offered a $50,000 prize (a fortune in those days) for the first person to fly across the Pacific Ocean—it went uncollected during his lifetime.

Nancy's father Thomas Harper Ince, Jr. was born in Hollywood, California. He was 12 years old when his father died. His mother wanted him to manage his father's production studio. Instead, he became a cameraman, a professional race car driver, a professional power boat racer, and a commercial fisherman. Although he wanted to be an Indianapolis race car driver, Thomas Jr. found most success in power boat racing. In 1944, Tom won the Hearst Trophy at Long

Beach Marine Stadium in the 225 hp engine class, making the front page of the *Los Angeles Examiner* Sports section.

Nancy's mother also had Hollywood connections — in a big way. She was born Dorothy Kitchen in New York in 1910. Her father was a New York fireman. When Dorothy was 15 years old, she won a beauty contest and a Hollywood contract. Her family wound up in Hollywood and soon her father — after retiring from the New York fire department with 20 years of service — went to work for Warner Brothers as Fire Chief for the studio. He remained on his new job for 37 more years. In 1926, Dorothy was put under contract by Universal Pictures where she acted in a series of comedies and westerns. She continued to play roles in the movies for various studios including Paramount, Fox, and MGM. In 1928, she changed her name to Nancy Drexel and continued in films until 1932 when she married Thomas H. Ince, Jr. and began to raise her family.

Nancy Norma Ince — whose middle name was in honor of another film star of the time and friend of the family Norma Talmadge — was born in 1933. It should also be noted that Nancy has a sister named Shirley — who is named after Shirley Temple. In spite of being surrounded

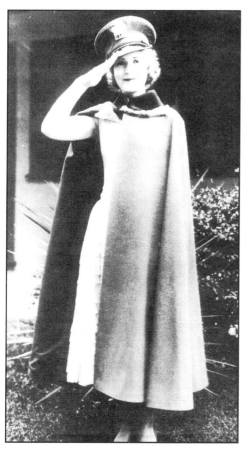

Nancy's mother, film star Nancy Drexel, in a movie role from 1928.

by show business, Nancy remembers that she was sheltered by her parents from the Hollywood scene. She spent much of her time as a young girl with her Irish maternal grandmother who liked to bet on horse races—and inspired Nancy's first interests in horses.

In addition to Hollywood, Nancy had Catalina connections. She remembers traveling to Avalon Bay on her father's yacht—a 40' ketch "*RIK*"—named after Richard Kershaw Ince—the brother who had died at an early age. She also remembers diving for coins when the Big White Steamer arrived at the Avalon Steamer Pier at noon each day in the summer season.

After Nancy graduated from South Pasadena High School, her family moved to a three story house on Olive Street in Avalon. Her first job after graduation was making flower leis for photographer Larry Creed in Avalon, who put them on tourists and took their pictures. She then decided to attend college on the mainland, so she moved to her grandmother's house in Palos Verdes. There she was able to ride her horse and attend USC where she studied art and English. After graduation from USC, she decided that she wanted to become a photographer or a stewardess.

In September of 1953 Nancy was headed to Avalon to visit her family. The boats serving the island could not make the transit because of rough water conditions, so she called her father to let him know. He recommended flying from the Long Beach airport on United Air Lines—so she headed for the terminal. She spotted the Avalon Air Transport counter—which had been in business for about one week—and decided to try them instead. Bob Hanley was the pilot of the Goose that headed for the island. When he arrived he decided that it was too rough to land on the water near Avalon, so he returned to Long Beach. Back at the airport, Dick Probert saw a challenge he could not refuse—a 20 year old co-ed and an ocean that someone else thought was too rough. So he made a Goose trip to the island which would change his life. On that flight he had a full load and asked Nancy to sit up front in the co-pilot's seat next to him. They made the open sea landing at White's Landing and, after taxiing on the wild open ocean for 45 minutes, they made it into Avalon Bay. And the rest, as they say, "is history."

Two years later, Nancy was hired by Walt von Kleinsmid as a ticket agent at Long Beach Airport for the summer season. She left her mark on passengers, the airport, and especially on Dick Probert. Her positive spirit and enthusiasm attracted island customers who would remain loyal throughout her entire airline career. She planted flowers in flower boxes at the Long Beach terminal and continued to spark the interest of Dick. Nancy's father noticed this association—and noting the age differences—told Dick to forget about her. To avoid conflict, Dick said *"OK, I'll write to her"* but privately confided while being interviewed for this book *"I didn't mean a syllable of it."*

With the addition of the Sikorsky flying boat to the AAT fleet in 1957, Nancy was the obvious choice to become the stewardess. As Dick said; *"I had a sweet young girl working for me on the passenger service counter at Long Beach airport who I assigned to the larger aircraft as cabin attendant."* For a ship the size of the four-engine flying boat, the FAA required a crew of pilot, co-pilot, and stewardess. What an addition to the flying boat she became. Wearing her sailor dress flight attendant uniform, a flower in her hair, and her radiant smile, she continued to charm passengers with her personal attention. She knew almost every islander by name and gave special service everywhere she could. The Dow family is one example. John, Muriel, and Tony Dow (star of the popular TV series *Leave It To Beaver*) owned a summer home in Avalon and were frequent travelers on the Sikorsky. Many times they would bring their pets. Sometimes it was the otter, the macaw, or the penguin. Nancy would use her grace and charm to blend this menagerie with the other 47 passengers—who just loved it. Can you imagine how this would be accepted today on an airplane trip?

Stewardesses have to be resourceful, and Nancy was a perfect example. She decorated the floating docks in Avalon with palm trees, balloons for birthday parties, and helped organize the Mariachi band to welcome visitors when exiting the flying boat at the Avalon docks.

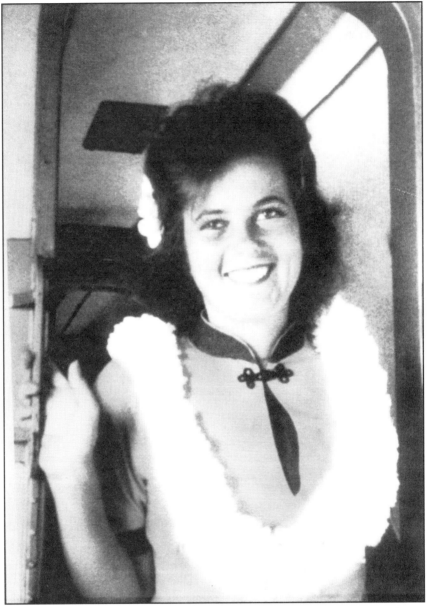

Nancy Ince greeted thousands of passengers flying on the Sikorsky VS-44A flying boat during the 1950's and 1960's wearing her flight attendant uniform, a lei, a flower, and her famous smile.

Part III — The Knights of Avalon

Nancy seated television star Tony Dow and his pet penguin when they traveled on the Sikorsky to Avalon.

Captain Dick Probert, Nancy Ince Probert, and Captain Lloyd Burkhard on the docks in Avalon bay.

Nancy would make sure that islanders who didn't like one another were not seated close together, and that cantankerous or inebriated passengers were dealt with smoothly. One summer, after 881 had been on a fishing charter trip to Ensenada, one of the fisherman's catch had slipped beneath floorboards where no one could reach it. To avoid potential passenger discomfort, immediately upon landing Nancy would quickly open the back passenger door to allow the smell of "the one that got away" to dissipate. This technique had to be employed for the good part of an entire summer season.

As Chief Stewardess, Nancy recorded 3,589 round trips during the 10 years that she served on the Sikorsky flying boat—thus claiming more takeoffs and landings than any other stewardess in history. This enthusiastic dynamo was married to Dick Probert in 1965. They have "retired" to their ranch—Rancho de los Avidores—along the northern California coast where they raise thoroughbred race horses. The ranch has an aircraft landing strip.

Warren Stoner

Warren Stoner was born in Kansas in 1915. When he was five years old, his father took him to a field where he took his first ride in an airplane with a barnstorming pilot. Airplanes would remain his first love from that day forward. When he was in high school he would hop on a local freight train to catch a free ride to the vicinity of the airport, where he would jump off. He would do anything to earn some money for rides and flight lessons—washing airplanes, sweeping out hangers, painting. One day, Warren missed the passing freight and was late getting to the airport for his scheduled flight lesson. When he arrived, he learned that the ship and his instructor had crashed, killing the student pilot. Undaunted, he continued until he was 17 years old when his family moved from Arkansas City, Kansas to Los Angeles, California. Warren immediately located the nearest airport—Metropolitan Airport in Van Nuys—where he met Dick Probert. Dick put this ambitious teenager to work and gave him flying lessons.

Part III — The Knights of Avalon

A young Warren Stoner with an OX-5 Travel Air.

To save travel time and money, Warren moved to the Van Nuys airport where he lived in the hanger with Dick Probert and his wife. Washing airplanes, sweeping out hangers, and other odd jobs combined to keep Warren in flying money. He also had some artistic talents which he used to great advantage. Before the days of electronic printing, poster art for the front of movie theaters was mostly done by hand—and here Warren excelled. In addition to theaters, Warren painted the signs, posters, and even the large logo that was displayed over the PSA flight school company hanger at the airport. Warren continued his flight training and ultimately flew his first solo flight in a very famous Curtiss "Robin."

In the late 1930's, Warren continued to work for Dick Probert and built up flight experience in a J-5 Travel Air. He remembered one particular trip where he ran out of gas in the air over Adrien, Texas. He landed in a farmers field, spent the night, and in the morning, he syphoned gasoline from the farmers tractor to continue the trip. It was also in the late 30's when Warren met his future wife, Alice. Alice remembers flying with Warren and during the flight as she looked down at the floor of the cockpit, she could see the ground below through a hole in the floor fabric covering. That didn't keep her from flying again many times with Warren—but she knew what kind of a man she was marrying.

Many life-long associations were connected through Dick Probert's aircraft operations in the San Fernando Valley. This was true both before the war, at Arlen-Probert, and after the war at Probert-Devine. Dick Probert, Warren Stoner, Alice Stoner, Fred Pierce—who will be profiled later, and Alice Pierce all enjoyed parallel experiences. Warren and Alice met in 1937, were married in 1939, and by 1940, both were working for Arlen-Probert Aviation.

This sign, painted by Warren, is an example of his artistic abilities. Poster art for theaters helped him earn extra income during the Depression to pay for his flight lessons.

At the start of WWII, Warren first tried to join the Army as a pilot and then he tried the Navy. He was refused by both however, because combat pilot applicants at that time were required to have completed 2 years of college. So Warren signed with the US Army Air Corps to serve as a flight instructor in Hemet, California. There, he and his good friend Fred Pierce spent much of the war training recruits to fly Ryan PT-22's and Stearman bi-planes. With the war winding down in April

The company hanger logo at Arlen-Probert Aviation Corporation was designed and painted by Warren — to earn money for pilot training.

Warren Stoner and Dick Probert with a J-5 Travel Air in Amarillo, Texas - October, 1937.

This aircraft was loaned to Warren for his solo flight by Douglas "Crash" Corrigan who later flew the same ship to Ireland in 1938. Corrigan's Transatlantic "mistake" flight was celebrated by a Depression weary world who cheered this audacious pilot on his 28 hour non-stop flight from New York to Dublin in the Irish Free State.

Denied by the US Bureau of Air Commerce to attempt a flight across the Atlantic in both 1936 and 1937, Corrigan was granted permission to fly from New York to California. After take off from New York, Corrigan headed east for Ireland rather than west — blaming a heavy cloud cover and his compass which "froze accidentally." He supposedly didn't realize his heading error until he touched down in Dublin. Upon return to the US, Corrigan promptly headed off on a 44 state tour celebrating his wrong way trip.

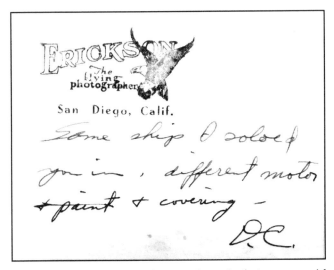

This is the back side of the photograph on the facing page, with a note from "Crash."

After Warren Stoner completed his first solo flight in a twin-engine Cessna, he displays the traditional chunk cut out of his shirttail following an old pilot ritual.

US Army flight school personnel at Hemet, California during WWII. Warren is in the front row, second from the left. His life-long friend and fellow instructor, Fred Pierce is in the back row, third from right.

of 1945, the pilot training center at Hemet was closed down and Warren went to Ft. Worth, Texas. He then began to train as a pilot for China National Airways, preparing to fly over the mountains in Burma ("the hump"). Before his training was complete, the war ended and his services were not needed.

After the war Warren took several flying jobs in succession. He instructed GI-Bill college students for Probert-Devine Aviation until it was forced to close in 1947. He flew for a construction company and also trained pilots in Tucson, Arizona. There he teamed with his friend Fred Pierce at Marana Airpark, training pilots for the US Air Force. In 1954, Warren worked for BLATS Airline. They flew DC-3's on various military contracts for the US Government. On one such flight, while he was laying over in Nashville, Tennessee, he received word that BLATS had been repossessed. At this point, something snapped. An inner voice told him that he needed to get out of flying. After an entire lifetime spent totally immersed in the world of aviation, he decided to

Part III — The Knights of Avalon

STUDENT MARILYN MOORE LIKES FLIGHT INSTRUCTOR STONER'S TECHNIQUE
But she and thousands of other GI flight trainees may be grounded by fund cut

This Los Angeles Daily News photo dated March 24, 1948 accompanied an article discussing the potential closing of flight schools funded by the GI Bill. The article goes on to state a "Typical GI school is the Probert-Devine operation at Whiteman Airpark in Pacoima, where some 150 students, including 10 women (ex-nurses from Birmingham Hospital) are in training."

make a complete change—something—anything not associated with airplanes.

Returning to his artistic side, Warren went to work for a house painting contractor back in the San Fernando Valley. No more moving or worrying about the vagabond life of an itinerant pilot. Alice went to work as a clerk at LA Valley College and they began to settle down and raise their son Chuck. After a couple of years, this semi-tranquil existence was interrupted when Dick Probert called to offer Warren a job with Dick's Avalon Air Transport. Warren wasn't quite yet ready to return to flying, so he took the job of Station Manager in Avalon.

Warren, Alice, and Chuck moved to Avalon, rented the house on Olive Street that had been owned by the Ince's and began to settle down on the island. Alice took a part-time job in Avalon at Rose's Rag Shop and Chuck was enrolled at Avalon High School. After a couple of seasons working in the airline office on the Pleasure Pier, Warren was again bitten by the flying bug. He decided to become a water pilot flying the Gooses from Long Beach. So, carrying an extra seat cushion—Warren wasn't all that tall—he had Dick Probert check him out and he began flying Goose operations to Catalina.

Not wanting to repeat the hectic existence he had lived when he was flying all over the country, Warren tried to make his new flying career resemble a "normal" day job. No more cross-country travel, living in motels, airplane hangers, or time spent away from his family. Now living in Long Beach, he could sleep in his own bed, eat meals at home, and live the good life. He also used his prior experience as the Avalon Station Manager to his advantage. When he would arrive at the Avalon base about lunch time, he would scan the passenger manifests to evaluate the flight schedule. He would then "volunteer" to take a particular flight to set himself up so that he would be the first pilot to finish for the day, and then he could go home early. He started to become such a home-body that fellow pilot Bill Kilgour referred to Warren as "Captain Daddy."

Captain Stoner was meticulous in his approach to flying—he wanted things to be just so. One bright summer morning, Warren was

Captain Warren Stoner at the controls of a Catalina Air Lines Grumman Goose. This was a familiar sight to thousands of islanders and tourists during the years he flew to the island.

sitting in his Goose at the seaplane floats in Avalon waiting for the dock boys to finish loading the passengers and luggage for departure. Suddenly, there was a commotion in the cabin of the Goose. One of the passengers—a rich yacht owner who had been drinking that morning—physically insisted on sitting in the exit seat by the door. This seat is near the stern of the ship and is usually reserved for a smaller and lighter passenger—which this yachtsman was not. The passenger occupying that seat was the priest from the Catholic church in Avalon, who had been asked to sit there by the dock boy at the door. Captain Stoner would not put up with this behavior on his airplane and he exploded. The yachtsman was deplaned (by the dock boy—with great difficulty) and was last seen storming onto a shore boat to return to his huge schooner moored at Casino Point. Stoner departed with one less passenger. In the meantime, the yachtsman had called Dick Probert on the mainland to complain.

Captain Probert showed up about 30 minutes later in another Goose. He radioed the Avalon base upon his approach and asked for a dock boy to meet him at the schooner with a skiff. As luck would have it, the same dock boy who had ejected the unruly passenger was now driving the boat. Fortunately, the yachtsman was too drunk to notice me although his sober wife gave me a knowing and apologetic smile as I buttoned up the Goose for departure from the open ocean near the yacht. In spite of—or because of—this type of professionalism and ability, many frequent flyers would request to ride with Captain Warren Stoner when they had their choice of Goose pilots.

After an illustrious career in aviation, Warren passed away in 1993. This man left many memories of his infectious laugh, booming voice, and enthusiasm. Warren Stoner was buried at sea. His ashes were spread from an airplane in mid-channel between the mainland and Catalina Island.

Fred Pierce

Fred Pierce was 4 years old when his parents emigrated to the United States from England. The family of five—older sister Irene, and younger brother George—docked in New York and they listed their names at Ellis Island. Fred's father and mother were both products of the Victorian age. It was a close family; his father was very "English" and certainly was the head of the household. He was strict and direct, but with a dry sense of humor. Fred was born in Liverpool, England in 1916, at which time his father was a pilot during World War I. However, Fred's father never discussed his role as a pilot during the war. In fact, his father did not want Fred to fly and discouraged his attempts.

As a boy, Fred was surrounded by exciting aviation events. He was 11 years old when Lindbergh flew the Atlantic and he was 12 when Amelia Earhart became the first woman to fly across the Atlantic. When he was 13, Fred's family moved to Van Nuys, California where his father took a job as a manager for Adohr Creamery Company in the LA Valley. Continuing his fascination with airplanes, Fred built balsa wood model airplanes as a teenager. In fact, his sister says that there were frequently 4 or 5 of his friends in his bedroom making models with him. They would sometimes crash them just to see how they performed. Later, Fred graduated to gas powered engines and then radio controlled models.

Fred had a funny, daredevil streak. He always seemed to be testing the limits. When he was 15 years old, his parents were gone from the house but had left the family Ford Model-T parked in the backyard. Fred wanted to test his driving skills so he took the T for a spin around the block. Fred drove out of the driveway and into the street. His brother and sister wanted to see him as he circled the block, so they ran to the back of the lot and waited for him to drive down the street at the back of the house. After a few minutes, he finally drove past. Upon return, when they quizzed him as to the delay, he explained that he had hit a fire hydrant and broke the windshield. Fred promptly

Fred Pierce in his Waco glider over the plowed fields of Van Nuys, California in the late 1930's. No one is sure who towed him up for his flights nor do they know how this picture was taken. Note the wingtip shoes and his seatbelt.

proceeded to get a hammer and break out all of the remaining glass fragments - leaving the windshield neat and tidy. The next morning, when Fred's father went out to drive the Model-T, he returned immediately to the house and asked *"Who broke the windshield"* to which Fred replied without hesitation *"I did."* His father, though stern, did not punish him for owning up to the misdeed right away. Another escapade that his sister remembers occurring is when the new Van Nuys City Hall building was under construction. Fred climbed the open steel girder frame to the top. It was the tallest structure around. Once there, some concerned citizens saw him and called the police because they thought someone was trying to commit suicide.

As a teenager in 1932, Fred went to the Whiteman Airport in Van Nuys to sign up for flying lessons from Dick Probert. Even though this

Warren Stoner approaches the twin-engine Cessna as Fred goes through his preflight routine. Warren had soloed this ship the same year and now he was training Fred so that he could be certified in twins, too.

was during the Depression and jobs were hard to come by, Fred did yard work and cleaned airplanes and hangers in order to earn enough money to get a 15 minute flying lesson. His sister Irene remembers Fred asking many times *"Sis, can you loan me $2 for a flying lesson?"* He would hitchhike to the airport for his lessons until he finally earned enough to buy a "jalopy" so he could drive there. After he graduated from Van Nuys High School he worked for Arlen-Probert Aviation and then went to work for the Lockheed aircraft factory. To keep in practice, he and a friend had a Waco Primary Glider that they flew. It had a 36' wing span, weighed 175 lbs., and it was red.

Soon after Great Britain and Canada entered the war against Germany in 1939, Fred joined the American Volunteer Group (AVG) contingent that went to Canada, where the Royal Canadian Air Force trained him to fly Hawker Hurricanes. His overriding motivation for joining up was to go to Europe to fight for his mother country England. However, after his training was complete, the RCAF wanted him to stay in Canada as a flight instructor rather than go to the war zone. Under a newspaper headline reading *"18 Veteran U.S. Fliers Trained to Train R.C.A.F."* ran a story dated September 16. In the article a spokesman for the group of fliers stated: *"They're going to a lot of trouble to give us this training. And it's certainly great of them. Everybody is fine to us up here, and we hope to prove our worth to the R.C.A.F."* The article continued: *"F.D. Pierce... will get fifty-two hours' special training—fifty of them in the air—on aerobatics, forced landings, instrument flying, navigation, formation flying, and night flying."*

Fred was based in Moose Jaw, Saskatchewan, Canada and his sister said that he used only one word in a letter home to describe his winter there *"COLD!!!"* One incident that she recalled was when a student gunner shot up the tail assembly of the training ship they were flying, but they landed safely. After Pearl Harbor, Fred transferred from the RCAF to the US Army Air Force and worked as a flight instructor with Warren Stoner at a base in Hemet, California. It was much warmer there.

During a leave from his wartime Air Force training duties, Fred had a blind date where he met a recently graduated Van Nuys High School student named Alice. In a whirlwind romance, Fred and Alice were married after 2 ½ months of courtship.

After the war, Fred went to work as a pilot for Probert-Devine Aviation Corporation at Whiteman Airport in Pacoima, California. He was flying a charter to Santa Barbara when an engine quit and he began to look for a clear place to land. His only choice was to set the ship down on the Pacific Coast Highway (Hwy 101). On his final approach to the highway, a lady in a station wagon came around a curve. Instead of continuing on forward under and away from the descending plane, she stopped dead in the middle of the road. Fred had no choice—on his right, power poles and wires lined the highway, and on his left was the rock-lined shore of the Pacific Ocean. He chose

Fred with his Hurricane fighter in Moose Jaw, Saskatchewan, Canada while on assignment for the American Volunteer Group with the RCAF. It was snowing lightly when this photograph was taken.

Stearman bi-planes were one type of aircraft used by Fred Pierce and Warren Stoner while instructing pilots for the Army in Hemet, California.

Fred and friends work on his gas powered control-line model plane. Fred enjoyed planes large and small.

the rocks and dumped it in. The only person hurt in the crash landing was Fred, mainly his face. Even the pregnant lady passenger in the plane was unhurt. She was so thankful that she and her unborn baby were unhurt that she called Fred for years after the crash to thank him.

One day at Probert-Devine a passenger walked up to the counter and chartered a plane, ostensibly for a local sight-seeing flight. Fred had just left on an emergency flight to deliver some medical supplies, so Dick Probert took the sight-seeing passenger up. As Dick climbed out above the Van Nuys area, his passenger asked him if he could fly higher so that he could be afforded with an even better view of the surrounding area. Dick complied and climbed the ship upward into the sky with his lone rider. Dick then noticed that the man had taken his wallet out of his pocket and was setting it on the seat. He then opened the door and jumped out! Later, during an interview, Fred showed his English dry wit once again when he commented on Probert making sure that he was paid for the charter flight. He said:

"If that suicide victim had not left his wallet on the seat, Dick would probably have dived after him."

After Probert-Devine had to close up shop because of the government reduction in flight training subsidies, Fred wound up working in Arizona. In the early 1950's Fred worked as a flight instructor at Marana Airpark, about a half-hour drive from Tucson. Exactly like his tour of duty in Hemet during the war, he again teamed with his friend Warren Stoner, where they both trained new pilots to fly. During this time Fred became a beer connoisseur. Although Alice remembers Fred being especially fond of apricot brandy—they even had a 17 year old white Persian cat named Brandy—Fred soon began to love beer just as well. After a hard day in the warm air over the desert, sweating with the maneuvers of pilot trainees, he and Warren faced a 30 minute car pool ride back home in the late afternoon heat. Rather than drive directly home, they would stop off at a local establishment while they waited for the temperature to drop some. Both men savored those days when they avoided the "heat."

Pilot training assignments took Fred Pierce (center - no hat) from Canada to California and from Arizona to Missouri.

In the latter half of the 1950's, Fred was working as an instructor at an Air Force Base in Missouri. One day the phone rang at home and Alice answered it. It was Dick Probert, who said *"let me talk to your old man."* He was inviting Fred to join him in flying for Avalon Air Transport. Fred had no water pilot experience, but DP had confidence in him and he knew that he could do it. So Fred moved his family to Naples, California where they initially stayed with the Stoners until they could get settled. There, Fred and Alice's daughter Susan could hang-out with Warren and Alice's son Chuck. Susan remembers flying to the island in a Goose with her Dad on many occasions. Fred rapidly became a very accomplished water pilot. Many times experienced Catalina islander passengers waiting to fly to or from the island would check to see what flight Captain Pierce was flying so that they could ride with him.

It was on Catalina Island where I got to know Fred, but his quiet demeanor, his wry sense of humor, and his infectious laugh concealed

Fred and Alice (foreground) at a New Year's Eve party.

his past. Like most of the classy people of his generation, he was humble and would not reveal his personal experiences without vigorous prompting. The stories included in this chapter were mostly recounted to me years later by his wife Alice, his daughter Susan, and his sister Irene. Fred had been a huge fan of Abraham Lincoln, Charles Lindbergh, and George Patton. The first two were humble and competent—the last one had a daring streak. Fred exemplified all of their attributes.

One day in Avalon Bay, Fred and I were swimming from the seaplane floats during the mid-day flight lull. I noticed some large scars on his body and asked *"Gees Fred, what the hell did you do to yourself?"* That was the day when he told me about his flight with the engine failure during the Santa Barbara charter flight. I had known Fred for about five years by then and he had never talked about himself. In a newspaper interview from the early 1970's, Captain Pierce said; *"A commercial jetliner would be boring work for me. But seaplanes are the only fun left in flying today."*

The last time that I was able to see and visit with Fred was at the Seaplane Reunion in Avalon in 1997. He came with his daughter Susan. Fred died at home of leukemia in 2000.

Jugs Burkhard

Lloyd Burkhard's father was born in Missouri in 1873 and was a farmer. His mother was born in India. They took the train in 1898 to Los Angeles where his father ultimately opened a grocery store in the suburb of Long Beach and his mother went to work for the Blue Seal Laundry Company. They both worked hard in those horse and buggy days, and by 1908 they owned a duplex.

Lloyd R. Burkhard was born on January 21st 1921 in Long Beach. He acquired many nicknames during his life including "Burkie" and (later) "Jugs" to emphasize his penchant for ladies of the top heavy persuasion. He worked in his father's grocery store as a bagger but he really wanted to fly an airplane. His father would not sign the permission slip for him to begin his lessons—but his mother did and he began flight training when he was in high school at the age of 15. He graduated from Long Beach Poly High School in 1939, and then began attending Occidental College while simultaneously taking flying lessons.

Some quotes from his Student Pilot Log Book shed some light on the type of young man we are dealing with here.

July 13, 1940 - W.C. Martin, Instructor Comments: *"Too confident"*

July 15, 1940 - Comments: *"Got slightly sick in spin stalls"*

With the outbreak of WWII, Jugs joined the US Navy and was sent to Pensacola, Florida for his military flight training. Upon graduation as a Flight Captain in November of 1942 at the age of 21, he was transferred to the Marine Corps where he began to fly DC-3's (R4-D4's)

Marine pilot Jugs Burkhard (seated) during a public relations interview by CBS Radio inside his transport during World War II. His trademark cigar is in his right hand.

and C-46's for the US Naval Air Transport Service in the Pacific. He flew to virtually all of the bases in the Pacific war zone including Guadalcanal, Kwajalein Atoll, Espirito Santo, and New Caledonia.

As a happy-go-lucky Marine in his early 20's, Jugs developed many habits when piloting these long, overwater freighter flights. First, he carried his flightbag/chartcase which he called his "brain bag." It included his flight charts of the Pacific, his navigation plotter, a prayer book that his mother gave him, and a .45 caliber sidearm. He also developed the flying habit of placing a large cigar in his mouth but not lighting it. Since the aircraft that he flew were usually filled with gasoline, bombs, and munitions it might be hazardous to everyone's health if he had a lit cigar so—no matches could be used onboard.

On one flight, nearing the Solomon Islands, Jugs was attacked by a flight of Japanese Zero fighters. Jugs put on his tin hat battle helmet, opened his pilot's window and began firing his .45 pistol at the attackers. A group of Grumman Wildcat fighters from the islands quickly arrived and took care of the Zeros. After landing in the islands, Jugs spent many days trying to find the Wildcat pilots to give them each some candy and cigars that he saved for special occasions such as this.

As pilot in command, Jugs took his duties very seriously and disregarding anyone's rank ran a tight ship. During a flight carrying a mixture of military brass and freight, one of his two engines malfunctioned and he was quickly losing altitude. In order to save his ship and passengers, he had to lighten the load by jettisoning some of his cargo. In selecting some heavy—but non-essential items—for pitching into the sea, he tossed one Colonel's personal case of booze in spite of the loud protestations of the Colonel. On another occasion, they were loading his ship on an island when the air-raid sirens started to sound. One passenger, a General, was slow to board the ship so Jugs promptly kicked him in the rear to hurry their departure before the impending enemy attack.

As you can imagine, it took some moxie to fly an (almost) unarmed cargo plane on long flights over the open sea knowing that there were armed enemies hunting for you. Jugs received two Air Medals for valor as a Naval Aviator while serving in the Solomon Island Area - they read as follows:

US Marine Corps Headquarters Aircraft Fleet Marine Force, Pacific -

> October 23, 1942 to November 2, 1942 - Air Medal for the *fifth flight in a combat area where enemy anti-aircraft fire was expected to be effective or where enemy aircraft patrols usually occurred.*

> November 2, 1942 to November 18, 1942 -Air Medal for the *sixth flight in a combat area where enemy anti-aircraft fire was expected to be effective or where enemy aircraft patrols usually occurred.*

After WWII, there was a great deal of civilian "general aviation" activity spurred by the high visibility of aircraft in the war and by the new GI Bill which provided funds for the flight training of veterans. Jugs returned to southern California and shortly began work as a flight instructor but he soon tired of the work and decided that he wanted to get away from flying, so he became a bouncer at the Long Beach Pike amusement park. This park had a world class roller coaster, cotton candy, sailors, locals, and girls—so you can imagine the skills that were needed to handle this job. Jugs was always "classily flamboyant" and he needed a car to match his personality—so he purchased a yellow 1946 Ford convertible with leopard spotted upholstery. As Jugs used to say *"It costs very little more to go first class."*

When it came to flying, Jugs was all business. He liked to say *"when I have an airplane strapped to my ass"* everything was by the book. But when not flying, Jugs had a very active sense of humor and he loved to laugh (roar) and to be with his flying buddies. He was known up and down the California coast as "El Lobo." One night at O'Shay's Bar in Belmont Shore—the only place with a TV in those days—he decided that he and his buddies would borrow the owner's TV set as a joke. Jugs worked out a diversion to facilitate the removal—he would stand up on the bar wearing only his briefs, flight jacket, and cigar. The heist plan failed miserably. As he mounted the hardwood bar wearing the appropriate outfit nobody paid any attention to him, because they knew Jugs.

Jugs returned to flying in the late 1940's and took just about any assignment using any type of aircraft that came along. He flew a crop duster—crashing with four chin scratches to show for it—and quit after two days. He flew a PBY Catalina for Van Camp Foods (tuna) to South America and back, carried vegetables from Mexico in a DC-3, captained a DC-4 to Paris, used a Beech-18 from Texas to Cuba for an oil company, and flew fire drop tankers in Arizona.

In 1948, Jugs met Dottie and married her the next year. Like everyone else in the Burkhard household, Dottie had a nickname— "Boots." While they were courting, Jugs (aka "Burk" or "Burkie") flew

Dottie Burkhard leans against a red Stinson in preparation for a flight with Jugs.

Lloyd Burkhard flew many types of aircraft to many different locations. Here, he is seen — on the right — riding a burro during a pack-trip to Mexico.

Jugs always drove a stylish vehicle.

Captain Burkhard in command of a Goose in Avalon bay for Avalon Air Transport.

a DC-3 charter from Long Beach to San Francisco and back. The point of the trip was to pick up a load of flowers for the return trip. With no other passengers, just the flowers, Jugs decided to take some friends along. Jugs also wanted to use the trip to check out his pilot friend Clarence Jasper in the DC-3. Jugs, Boots, and Jas were returning from San Francisco when the weather turned nasty. As Jugs set up for the instrument landing in the terrible weather conditions, he said to the others *"if we die, at least we will have a nice funeral."*

By 1950, Jugs and Boots had a baby daughter, Frances, who was nicknamed "Tootie" after "the little engine that could." Five years later, a son named Lloyd (nicknamed "Button" because of his button-like nose) was born. Clarence Jasper was his Godfather. As "Button" grew up he worked for a time at both the San Pedro and Pebbly Beach seaplane bases as a ramp agent during the 1970's. Because of his large

"Jugs" Burkhard was a competent and enthusiastic pilot for AAT and CAL during the 1950's and 1960's—no matter what type of aircraft he was flying.

size and rather subtle "speed" rating, his co-workers gave him another nickname—"Lightning."

By the mid-1950's, Jugs began flying a Grumman Goose for Dick Probert to Catalina Island. Sometimes, Hollywood personalities would contract for charters and, on one, Jugs flew a Goose to Lake Tahoe carrying the "Rat Pack" with Frank Sinatra in the right seat, Sammy Davis, Jr., and Peter Lawford. Jugs was a smooth pilot and he prided himself on making smooth landings. When he had successfully touched down and landed with all the grace of a bird he would sometimes pick up the pilots microphone and simply say to the station personnel "tweet-tweet."

When the giant four-engine Sikorsky flying boat was added to the Avalon Air Transport fleet the six day a week pilot was Dick Probert. Captain Probert was required by the FAA to take one day off each week, so Dick usually choose Jugs to replace him as the pilot-in-command. For the 10 years that the Sikorsky VS-44A flying boat was owned by Probert (1957-67), he trusted his "baby" with Jugs. Jugs' flight logbook for September 9, 1957 reads: *first flight with 881 - co-pilot 50 minutes - local*. Jugs really enjoyed the trust and the responsibility of flying the Sikorsky but he still retained his fertile and warped sense of humor. During one practice flight - just to shake up the air traffic controllers in the tower at the Long Beach airport - he radioed for clearance to land the big seaplane. One can only imagine the looks and the thoughts of the tower operators when the big bird skimmed just over the runway during the low pass with no landing gear.

Jugs Burkhard was a classic pilot who had earned the ultimate—a multi-engine sea rating. During his career, he logged more than 10,000 total hours in the air with over 500 of those hours spent flying over the open ocean. He especially loved to fly the big flying boat. His logbook entry after the sale of the Sikorsky reads: *"Probert retired, airplane sold to Charlie Blair, Son of a Bitch!!!*

Clarence Jasper

Flight Lieutenant Clarence Jasper of RCAF Squadron 418 was returning to his fighter base in southern England from a Daylight Ranger mission over Germany when his observer/navigator spotted the Junkers JU-88 bomber. It was June 27, 1944 and "Jaz" was flying the lead position in a two ship flight of DeHavilland Mosquito fighter/bombers. His wing man during this high speed, tree top patrol was Squadron Leader Russell Bannock (later to become one of the top Canadian aces of WWII), who was flying his first Daylight Ranger mission. They were just leaving the continent of Europe and entering the airspace over the Baltic Sea when the bomber was sighted just off the coast from Rostock, Germany. The German twin-engine bomber was about two miles ahead and slightly above their position.

As they maneuvered to a firing position below and behind the "88" they were spotted by the crew of a German passenger liner that was slightly further out to sea. The ship began sending up flares as a warning to the Ju-88 pilot who responded by maneuvering almost directly over the ship, which was well equipped with 40mm anti-aircraft batteries. Jaz pulled up into a 20-degree climb and continued to close on the Junker. At gunnery school Jaz had been told, "It will be to your advantage not to open fire, when using cannon, at a range less than two hundred yards." At a range of about 75 yards, Jaz opened fire with a two-second burst from his 20mm cannon and his .303-inch machine guns.

The following text is quoted from Eric Hammel's *Aces at War: The American Aces Speak*, volume IV. Published by Pacifica Press, Pacifica, CA., 1997.

"I saw strikes on both wing roots, and the port engine burst into flames, followed almost immediately by the starboard engine. A violent explosion then took place; the Ju-88 exploded in a huge cloud of flame, and flaming pieces fell into the sea over a wide area. I pulled through to starboard, but I could not avoid flying through the flames and debris. After emerging, I looked

at my left wing, which was burning like a Yule log, and thought, "Jaz, you stupid bastard, you really blew it this time." We were too low to bail out, and ditching in the Baltic Sea is very non-habit forming due to the temperature of the water.

In a very few seconds, the fire burned out, but the rudder pedals were vibrating badly. I thought of heading to Malmo, Sweden, which was about 70 miles away, but after checking the engine instruments and seeing that everything was working normally, I elected to head for home. Crossing 300 miles of the North Sea gets your attention. That water is rough even in good weather. We flew on to our squadron's base at Holmsley South and landed at 2113 hours. After touching down, I found directional control a little tricky. By using light touches of brake differentially, I managed to keep the airplane in a straight line.

After getting out of the airplane I could see why I had problems. The fabric was burnt entirely off the rudder, as was a large strip of fabric on the port side of the fuselage and a smaller piece of the port wing. Fortunately, control surfaces other than the rudder were metallized."

Not much is known about Clarence Murl Jasper. He was a modest man, he didn't talk much, and he didn't have any children. He was medium sized, well muscled, had a ruddy face, a large white bushy mustache and a "happy to be alive" attitude. He rolled his own cigarettes.

Jaz was born about 1915 and served in the US Navy during the middle 1930's where he became the heavyweight boxing champion on a Navy cruiser in 1938. He left the US Navy, took flying lessons, and when the war broke out in Europe, he decided to join the Royal Canadian Air Force in 1940. He earned his wings in 1942, became a flight instructor for the RCAF and in October 1943 he transferred to Mosquito flight training. By December, he was assigned to combat flight duties in England.

The Mosquitos he flew were a lot of airplane. Constructed primarily of plywood, this twin-engine fighter/bomber was capable of around 450 mph—the fastest piston engine aircraft of the Second World War. Jaz's fighter group the 418 "City of Edmonton" Squadron

Clarence Jasper became an ace flying the DeHavilland Mosquito fighter-bomber based in England. These ships were the fastest piston-engine aircraft in the war.

was given free reign with these DeHavillands throughout enemy occupied Europe to select any enemy target of opportunity. In addition to high speed Daylight Ranger intrusions, the Mosquitoes of the 418th also flew "Flower" Night Ranger intruder missions. Unlike nightfighters, which were in the business of intercepting the enemy bombers attacking England, these missions were to intercept the enemy bombers as they were returning to their respective bases, and, hopefully, to keep the enemy night-fighters on the ground when the RAF was bombing Germany. Each Mosquito was a predator on its own. They patrolled in the dark near Luftwaffe airfields, radar beacons, bomber streams—just about anywhere they felt that they would find an enemy aircraft.

Flying his Mosquito during 1944, Jaz shot down six German planes in the air, destroyed four on the ground and destroyed three V-1 buzz bombs in the air. Combat tactics for shooting down an unmanned V-1 pulse-jet were different from those employed against enemy fighters and bombers. The V-1's were usually programmed to fly at or below

Captain Jasper flew Gooses to Catalina for many years. During that time, the name and paint scheme for the airline changed several times.

3,000 feet and their speed was about 370 mph. Jaz would patrol at about 10,000 feet until he spotted a buzz bomb. He would then dive at the V-1 aiming for a location just behind and below. Timing was everything for this manoeuver because if you shot and exploded the bomb directly in front of you, you would be included in the explosion and resulting destruction. The trick was to shoot at the bomb from an angle until it erupted and then immediately turn and dive away from the blossoming and flaming debris. Credit for a V-1 kill was given to a pilot if he shot it down *before* it made it to the British Isles. If the pilot made the kill *over* the islands, he was only given ½ a kill credit.

Clarence Jasper's six aerial victories, four ground victories, and three V-1's killed made him an Ace and earned him the Distinguished Flying Cross.

During his life, Jaz had three wives. His first wife was killed in their London apartment in a German bombing raid during the Blitz. Following the war, he married his second wife (Jeannie) but she died from complications caused by diabetes. Throughout her illness, Jaz had carefully helped her with taking her shots at the proper time and with her diet. Jaz married his third wife Mozelle and they lived in a beautiful home in Long Beach, California near the Long Beach traffic circle where his favorite hobby was tending his garden and landscaping. Mozelle died in Long Beach of bone cancer. After her death, Jaz found that he couldn't pilot a plane because of his nerves and sorrow.

Upon discovering Jaz's plight, his friend Fred Pierce made up a story that convinced Jaz to go with Fred on a charter flight he was piloting. As the chartered plane was returning empty, Fred took his hands off of the controls and told Jaz to take over the controls or they both were going to crash. That snapped Jaz out of his flying difficulties and Jaz began to fly again. Clarence Jasper was my first pilot, he was the Godfather to Button Burkhard, and he was a man to be admired by all. He was a man of immense depth and character—always positive and highly competent. As Fred Pierce's widow said to me during an interview about Jaz 20 years after his death *"He was a wonderful, wonderful, kind man."*

PART IV — Adventures in Paradise

> *"If it moves, kiss it, if it doesn't move, paint it."*
>
> - A dock boy saying

Clear— right!!! Yelled the dock boy as he scanned for boat traffic in the bay. Captain Stoner hit the switch for the right radial engine, there was a slight high-pitched whine as the starter engaged and then the engine sputtered. Finally, it roared to life and the three-bladed prop began to fan the air - then he repeated the sequence for the left engine on his fully loaded Grumman Goose.

The two bikini-clad young women leaning against the silver railing at the top of the green Avalon pleasure pier watched the sea/airship as it began its voyage across the San Pedro Channel to Long Beach airport - about a 15-20 minute flight. Sunlight reflecting off the surface of the bay dazzled the women who watched the scene. They were more interested, however, in the tanned muscular dock boy who deftly moved around and under the propeller, wing, and tail of the Goose as the tie down ropes were released - launching the combined 900 horsepower craft on its journey. The bright summer sun glinted off the white, blue, and red amphibian as it gracefully slipped away from the floats in the middle of Avalon Bay and began to taxi through the gauntlet of pleasure boats sprinkled across the mouth of the harbor on this busy Sunday in Paradise.

Captain Stoner let his ship turn into the prevailing northwest wind. After checking once again for boat traffic, and then for any traffic in the air, he slid both throttles full forward. The three-bladed props bit into the wind as the two throaty 450 hp Pratt-Whitney radials spooled up quickly to their distinctive mellow roar, muffled by the surrounding sea, spray, and salt air. The Goose quickly went from a fish to a bird.

The realm of the dock boy.

The dock boy ambled up the 100' of floats to the benched waiting area, took off his shirt, and stretched out on a white bench to catch some sun rays and wait for the next ship to appear on the horizon. The two women then returned to the sandy beach on the frontstreet - wondering what party they might try for that evening.

The Goose continued to climb gracefully trailing salt spray from its hull and floats as it turned slightly to the right for the proper heading –direct to Long Beach airport for a landing on dry land. With the takeoff complete, Captain Stoner then retracted the pontoon flip-floats to their cruising locations at the end of each wing. For his next return to Avalon Bay, Captain Stoner would redeploy the wing floats to their down position upon his approach for landing. On a busy summer day, he would probably log between 10 and 14 round trips in his Grumman Goose.

A Dock boy Morning

The main action during the 1950's and 1960's in Avalon Bay occurred right in the middle – on the Pleasure pier. From this location, daily occurrences were turned into entertaining events. When a marlin boat returned from a successful trip, the Harbor Master would fire his cannon to attract attention. Every time a Goose or the Sikorsky landed or took off they attracted attention. These events made noise and they were flashy. The same might be said for the dock boys of Catalina Air Lines. They were exactly in the center of the action, the interface between the aircraft and the island, they too were noisy and flashy. Let's look at a typical day in the life of a dock boy. The typical day really began the night before, but I digress.

Miraculously, you would wake up – normally at home – in time to dress and run down to the end of the pier to punch in on the time clock located on a small back shelf in the airline office. On the way down the pier, you could see the same handful of elderly gentlemen engaged in their daily morning ritual at the pier hamburger stand. They would start the day with a stiff "coffee royal," and then, by the time we came by, they would have already discussed the news events of the day and were starting their game of checkers. And we weren't even fully awake yet.

During the summer season, there were usually about 8 dock boys employed at the seaplane base. Virtually every one of them was a college student on summer vacation. Dock boy duties included: a six day work week, usually from 7:30 am to 8:00 pm. During that time you wore your dock boy uniform – a blue airline shirt with white letters that spelled out Catalina Air Lines on the back, white (not counting the oil spots) Bermuda shorts, and Topsider deck shoes. Topsiders were for traction on the wet docks and in the boats – you could count on having to replace them at least once during a summer of wear, tear and saltwater.

Routine dock boy duties each morning included: bucket rinsing of the floats with seawater, bailing out and unchaining the two skiffs that were attached to the floating docks, mounting and testing the outboard motors, unchaining all four of the wheeled baggage carts (used for hauling the luggage, freight, and mail up and down the ramps from the pier to the floats), and hoping that you were finished early enough to enjoy the donut and coffee that you picked up on your way down to the pier. The donut shop was extremely popular. It featured excellent coffee and a well rounded selection of maple bars, Bismarcks, jelly-filled, etc. This was the shop of choice (for those with the time to stop off) on the way to work on the floats.

A brief word about island housing for summer employees: as noted earlier, the town of Avalon was extensively developed beginning at the start of the 20th century. Most of the apartments available to summer workers originated at that very time. Housing was very small, crowded to within about three feet of the house next door, and not very well insulated. Avalon is at 33° north latitude—generally warm most of the year. If a party was held in one of these summer domiciles, it could lead to some complaints from neighbors who needed their sleep. The first "house" that I stayed in had basically three rooms. A combination living room, dining room, kitchen; a tiny bathroom, and one small bedroom. There were five of us sharing this abode (you can imagine the stress on the bathroom - or even the tiny refrigerator). Our landlord had taken the trouble to satisfy two needs at the same time. He had covered the main room walls with record album covers from the big band era (mostly Russ Morgan). This helped with the decor and possibly deadened the sounds emanating to our close-by neighbors. It also gave me the feeling that we were not the first to enjoy the charms of the island (or this apartment either).

Another year, with a couple of other roommates, I rented an apartment right on the Steamer Pier. What a location! We were two steps from all of the action on the main street of Avalon—Crescent Street. The apartment was located over the shore-break and we could hear the waves at all times—talk about atmosphere! A major benefit was that if we overslept in the morning, we could hear the first amphibian flight approaching the dock on the other pier. We would throw on our uniforms, and only have about a two hundred yard run to punch in.

Part IV — Adventures in Paradise

The first flight from the mainland each morning was a Goose from Long Beach airport. It would (except for the early bird flight on Monday mornings) depart LGB (the three letter international designation for that airport) at 8:00 am and arrive at AVX (Avalon Bay) at 8:20. This flight carried the US mail and the first wave of returning islanders and tourists for the day. We prided ourselves on expediting the mail to the Avalon Post Office at top speed. Anyone on the beach, Crescent Street, or in the alley behind the Post Office would see at least one — sometimes more — baggage carts loaded with large grey mail sacks careening around corners with a dock boy hanging on. There were several reasons for this display of haste. First, we wanted to keep our reputation for promptness and avoid the displeasure of the Post Master, his employees, and most importantly the island residents. The mail was traditionally available to islanders in their Post Office boxes for pick-up around noon each day. Islanders are in a unique situation, and can be quite finicky about contact with the outside world — they are basically captives of geography, and although never officially stated, this condition is the backdrop for all thoughts and actions.

A brief word about the mail. Receiving mail is a very important part of feeling that you are part of and connected to the rest of the world. Islanders get very testy if their mail is late. The Post Master knows this too. He needs time to un-sack, sort, and distribute the mail to the proper boxes. There is no delivery on the island - only PO boxes.

Early in the history of Avalon Air Transport, Dick Probert and Walt von Kleinsmid contracted with the US Postal Department to deliver the mail to Avalon. This contract was easily fulfilled each day by putting the two or three grey canvas sacks of regular mail and one orange nylon sack of air mail on the first Goose flight into Avalon and sending the outbound mail on the 4:30 pm flight to Long Beach. It should be noted that ALL of the mail going to and from the island was airmail. However, that was only one leg of that piece's journey. Any piece stamped airmail would go in the orange nylon airmail sack (instead of dirty grey for regular mail), and it would travel by air all the way to or from its final destination. Otherwise, a piece of mail with regular postage would only cover the twenty six miles by air. From then on to the recipient, it would stay in the dirty grey sack and go slower.

After the dock boys delivered the mail to the Avalon Post Office, it was time to return to the floats to finally consume the donut shop items previously purchased. Another postal sidelight occurred once a year when the Sears catalogs were sent to Avalon. This event was looked upon by the islanders and the dock boys from opposite perspectives. The islanders eagerly awaited the arrival. It was akin to another TV channel being added to your station lineup—pure enjoyment and entertainment. Dock boys saw the catalog season differently. The maximum weight of a mail sack in those days, was about 70 or 75 lbs. These sacks are made of heavy canvas and have no handles. About twenty sacks of catalogs made up a normal annual shipment. This filled the bow and cabin of two Gooses. Just loading —at the Long Beach airport—and unloading these heavy sacks was tough—not to mention the loading onto carts, pushing them up the ramp to the pier and then to the Post Office where they were stacked waiting for the happy islanders to peruse.

It should also be mentioned that the stage of the moon—and, therefore, the height of the tide—had a great effect on this whole procedure. Anyone who has gone to the seashore to catch crabs or dig for clams knows that the tide goes in and out twice a day. During certain times of the year, because of the pull of the moon, there are extra high and low tides at the island's latitude. When this occurs, the ramps between the pier and the floats become almost level (a plus high tide) or almost vertical (a minus low tide). Hard as it is to believe, the US Postal Service was able to coordinate the delivery of the Sears catalogs with the minus low tide in Avalon bay every year.

Docking 881

Some jobs during the course of the day were more of a challenge than others. Driving one of the skiffs to dock the Sikorsky flying boat was one of the most rewarding. Docking 881 was an adventure that happened several times each day. Basically, what we tried to do was lasso the ship with a couple of ropes, turn it around and then slide it up against the floats where people, luggage, and freight could be transferred.

This exercise was akin to maneuvering your local JC Penny store through its own parking lot—full of cars—and then plunking it down where it belonged. Let me explain:

First of all, the ship itself is HUGE, the top of the vertical stabilizer is 27' (taller than a 3 story building), the wingspan is 124' (about the size of two standard size houses), and the length of the ship is 76'. For directional control on the water, it should be remembered, the Sikorsky had 4 engines and the wing and tail surfaces only. That meant no brakes, no reverse, and not even a water rudder... after engine shutdown, she was at the mercy of the wind and waves.

In order to get this big ship to the dock in the middle of the bay— through all of the usual small boat traffic— it took a little planning and execution. First, let's examine the tools used by the dock boys for the airline operation in Avalon bay.

- A "pivot line" attached to some railroad wheels at the bottom of the bay. This line had Styrofoam floats at the top end so that it would not sink.
- Two skiffs; the "Woody" boat - a 16' wooden boat with an 18 hp outboard motor, and the "Tinny" boat - a 14' aluminum boat also with an (usually) 18 hp outboard motor.
- One 100' length of 1" nylon line with a large snap hook at one end - this was the "tail line".
- A number of dock boys (from 1 to 8) to drive the boats, pull on the lines, and finally, to tie up the big ship.

After the ship landed just outside Avalon Bay, she would taxi carefully through the boats in the bay toward the docks. The pilot of the Sikorsky (usually Dick Probert, sometimes Jugs Burkhard, and occasionally John Pinney) would shut down the two inboard engines

The Sikorsky, with only the right outboard engine running, slowly approaches the Tinny boat. The co-pilot of 881 is extending a boat hook from the bow hatch of the flying boat. The author is the driver of the Tinny boat, the man holding the pivot line is David Turner.

and control the ship using the two outboard engines only. Dick Probert had the mechanics drop the outboard engines idle speed to only 400 rpm to allow for a slower taxi speed. The Sikorsky would approach the Tinny boat which held two dock boys. One was the driver, the other dock boy would hand the pivot line to the co-pilot who was located in the bow hatch and held a boat hook. After the hand-off, the Tinny boat driver would then turn toward the docks and drop off the other dock boy who would wait to pull on the tail line.

The Woody boat also held two dock boys. One was the driver, and the other would attach the snap hook on the tail line to a large ring located on the lower tail section of the flying boat the driver of the Woody boat would chase the stern of the fast-taxiing flying boat in order to catch up with the stern—the Woody boat was much heavier and slower than the tinny boat. The Woody boat driver would then turn toward the docks and drop off the other dock boy who would wait to pull on the tail line. With both the pivot line and the tail line attached, the Sikorsky pilot would usually shut down all engines—counting on the wind, swells, skiffs, lines, and dock boys to safely nudge the ship against the dock.

David Turner prepares to start the Woody boat while Bob Frost (also nicknamed Woody) gets set to help him cast off from the summer floats.

Depending on the wind direction and velocity, the two skiff drivers would position their boats on the downwind side of the Sikorsky hull and begin to *gently* push on the ship where needed. Both boats had padding (an old aircraft tire - cut in half - and fastened to the bow) on the nose to avoid damaging the sheet-aluminum sides of the flying boat. This entire operation was somewhat similar to a water ballet—the flying boat would pivot on the pivot line, slide backward along the dock being pulled by the tail line, and then when in about the right position the pivot line (attached to the railroad wheels on the bottom of the bay) was exchanged for a shorter bow line that was attached to the dock. Both lines were then snugged up and the process was complete. All hatches were opened and the exchange of passengers and luggage began.

This docking exercise was usually performed 6 to 8 times a day—sometimes more than twice that on a busy summer Saturday and Sunday. Total turnaround time was about 10 to 20 minutes - depending on several variables: the number of passengers to load/unload, the amount of luggage and freight, wind and water conditions, small boat traffic, number of dock boys available (and hangover quotient). Some days with 881 were special—Sundays, Wednesdays, and Jugs Burkhard days for instance:

Sundays -

> On Sundays, there was no freight, no mail, and relatively few passengers from the mainland. Most folks were completing their holiday on Sunday and were returning home to start their workweek the next day. So this was a day where, as a dock boy, you could somewhat relax and simply herd passengers and luggage all day with little chance of over-stressing your work shorts. Always looking for a diversion, dock boys decided that they would wear a special uniform on Sundays - to add to the festive atmosphere of the islands and the tourists' enjoyment on their departure. A then current fashion fad was imported from the

N41881 at the dock in Avalon.

Part IV — Adventures in Paradise

A Sunday picture—"Jams Day"—with our shirts on backwards so that everyone would know who we worked for. Front row l-r: David "DJ" Johnston (who sneezed just as this shot was taken), John Lewis, Tom "Devil Eyes" Davoli, Bill "Stork" Harvey. Back row l-r: Mike Harris, David "DT" Turner, Greg "Mad Gorgen" Madden, and Greg "Babe Magnet" Harris. The locker that the back row is standing on is called "the coffin," it held ropes, oars, and other dock boy supplies.

Hawaiian Islands - Jams. Short for pajamas, Jams were light-duty Bermuda shorts that were created using Hawaiian Island floral patterns. The louder - the better. We thought they were beautiful, and they gave dock boys at least one reason to look forward to Sundays.

Wednesdays -

Every Wednesday was freight day. Remember that there are no bridges to the island—and most things come from the mainland by boat. Boats (and barges) provided cheaper shipping costs for businesses, but they were too slow for shipping some items. Meat, frozen foods, and bakery goods were shipped by plane. Sometimes, the Grumman Gooses were used (in the winter, etc.),

A former Pan American Airways employee, who used to work on the Pacific route, took this picture in 1963. Boxes of fresh meat are stacked topside after being pulled from the port wing bins. The boxes on the starboard wing are frozen foods. On the docks are Rick "ValowEyes" Valois, Tim "Timmy" Evans, David Johnston (catching boxes). On the wing are David Turner, Joe (Udo) "The Alien" Waldman - from Sweden, and Tom Flood. Note that there are two boxes in the air at the same time.

but the Sikorsky had two huge bow compartments, 8 wing bins, and a tail section that were perfectly suited for hauling freight.

Early on Wednesday mornings, the frozen food would be delivered to the Long Beach harbor seaplane base at Pacific Landing. This base was where the HMS *Queen Mary* is now on permanent display. There, the LBH dock boys would carry the boxes down the ramp and onto the dock. Then the boxes were loaded into the bow compartments and wing bins by tossing each one from man to man. In Avalon Bay, the process was reversed—with some additional duties for the dock boys in Avalon. Where the LBH dock crew had about an hour to load the freight, in Avalon the Sikorsky had to be turned around within 20 minutes. That meant that 8 dock boys needed to dock the Sikorsky, unload everything, load the passengers and their bags that were returning to the mainland, and usually "spin" a Goose or two from the end of the dock—in between times. Being in some sort of good physical shape was somewhat mandatory.

Jugs Burkhard Days -

On those occasional days when Jugs Burkhard flew 881, the dock boys loved it. Without Dick Probert flying, we could count on there being no maintenance edicts. Owner Probert loved his airline—and 881 even more—so on those days when he was flying he always seemed to have a task or two for the dock boys to keep everything shipshape. When Jugs stepped off of 881—actually, sometimes he would exit through the pilot's window and slide down the side of the flying boat—he would be wearing his signature Hawaiian hat, light up a big cigar, and say to the boys on the floats *"Howdy Amigos!!!"* He then would proceed down the Pleasure Pier to the beach—to see what views there were to behold. To the dock boys in Avalon, Jugs was an impressive figure—a tall, tanned, eminently likeable man who looked like a movie star but with no false airs about him.

One never knew what Captain Jugs Burkhard might do next. This photo is from his pre-mustache days coming out of the pilots hatch on the Sikorsky.

Particularly enjoyed by the dock boys on Burkhard days were the opportunities for the sought after "single boat hookup" (and single boat/single man hookup). Let me explain:

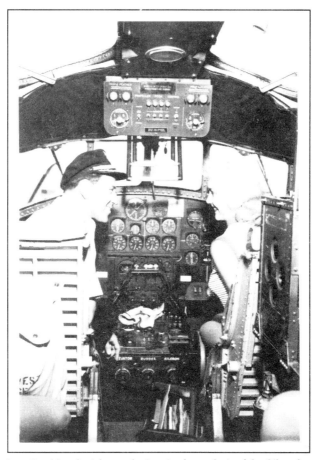

Jugs Burkhard with an admirer in the cockpit of the Sikorsky.

The standard docking procedure as outlined earlier, became boring and routine after a while. So, always looking for some excitement, the dock boys designed the single boat hookup. Actually, this single boat procedure was born of necessity when, at different times, some problem or condition precluded the use of two boats. One of the boats could be temporarily out of commission with a bad engine, a leak, or perhaps there were not enough dock boys to man two boats. They might be off delivering mail or, on some occasions, they hadn't been bailed out of jail yet from the prior night's activities.

Here's how the single boat docking procedure worked: The Sikorsky would taxi up to the one boat which held two dock boys, the bow line, and the tail line. The boat driver would wait for the other dock boy to hand the pivot line to the co-pilot. The boat driver would then turn and head for the tail of 881 (which was still moving - the two outboard engines were just shutting down). There, the tail line/snap hook would be quickly attached to the ring on the underside of the tail.

Then the driver would wheel back to the docks and drop off the other dock boy, who would jump out with the end of the tail line and begin to pull on it. The single boat driver would then circle around to the downwind side (starboard) of 881 and push—if needed. As 881 slid backward along the dock, the pivot line was exchanged for the shorter bow line that was attached to the dock. These lines were then snugged up and tied fast.

There was also a single boat/single man docking. This was just the same as the above procedure except the boat held only one man who performed all of the tasks. This technique was saved for rare occasions when there was little wind, no other boat traffic, Jugs was flying, and the dock boy was gutsy enough to try it.

Sometimes, the dock boys would play with the mind of the pilot (Jugs - definitely not Probert). The single boat hookup would work as outlined before - except the dock boys would be wearing huge, floppy sombreros, and would be reclining on their backs—feigning sleep until just before the co-pilot—with his boat hook at the ready—was on top of the single boat. The dock boys would then leap up and perform their proper duties (to be ready - the boat engine was kept idling). Only Jugs had enough moxie to let these 18-22 year old dock boys play with the fate of a 50,000 lb airplane and its contents. He had enough faith in his own abilities (and hopefully in the dock boys) to extricate everyone from any trouble - should it arise.

The Glass Bottom Boat

For most of the 20th century, Avalon Bay had two piers, the Pleasure Pier and the Steamer Pier. The Pleasure Pier was constructed in 1909, and it continues to host the following activities: the Chamber of Commerce office, Eric's hamburger stand, Joe's Rent-a-Boats, scuba diving rentals, and at the water end of the pier, the Avalon Fish Market, and the Harbor Master's office. In addition, there are shore boats for transporting boat owners to and fro, and a very large hoist for raising and lowering things. The main summer use for the hoist is lifting marlin out of sportfishing boats. The fish are then weighed on the scales next to the hoist. When the Harbor Master, from high-atop the pier, spots a fishing boat entering the harbor flying a marlin flag, he fires a small cannon — signaling the catch to locals and tourists alike. The crowd then assembles around the hoist to watch the weighing and photographing ceremonies.

The second pier — the Steamer Pier — had been the docking location for various large commercial steamers beginning in the middle of the 1800's. In 1848, California (and Santa Catalina Island) become part of the United States by treaty with Mexico. After the US civil war, various ships sailed to this pier. Old photographs from that era show a lonesome steamer at the pier, one hotel, and a very small scattering of houses and tents. During the time (1864 - 1887) that the island was owned by the James Lick Trust (of Lick Observatory fame), the side-wheeler ship "Amelia" began transporting passengers to the pier. An interesting side note, its purser was William Banning, who with his brothers, became the owner of the island in 1891. After the purchase, the Bannings began development of the city of Avalon as a destination resort. They sold lots in Avalon, and constructed a hotel. In 1896, they formed the Santa Catalina Island Company, and began to use the steamer pier for the glass bottomed row boats that were used to observe the unique marine gardens just to the east of Avalon bay. From 1923 to 1975, the steamship "SS *Catalina*" (307" long with capacity for 1,963 passengers) docked at the steamer pier as it provided summer service from San Pedro to Avalon.

Part IV — Adventures in Paradise

The glass bottom boat Phoenix *has just backed away from the Steamer Pier and is heading in front of the Sikorsky for the undersea gardens in Lover's Cove.*

Today, glass bottom boats remain a major tourist attraction on the island. You may recall seeing the movie *"The Glass Bottom Boat"* a 1966 production starring Doris Day and Rod Taylor. Arthur Godfrey played Miss Day's father and the captain of the Glass Bottom Boat. During the production company filming, a trench was dug on the beach near the Pleasure Pier. In order to simulate that the boat had run aground at top speed, they merely placed the boat at the top of a trench.

For many years, Eddie Harrison was the Captain of the large double-decked, paddle-wheeled glass bottom boat named the *"Phoenix."* Captain Harrison is the father of the movie actor—Gregory Harrison, who grew up in Avalon. Captain Harrison was very proud of his role in command of this large and important craft and he wasn't about to let anything interfere with his mission. As you can imagine, there was a clash with that other large and important craft that operated in the bay during the 1950's and 60's—the Sikorsky VS 44A piloted, by another strong personality—Dick Probert. In order for these two to get to their respective destinations, they had to cross each other's paths (sometimes - several times a day). The *Phoenix*, being a powered ship, had a reverse gear; the Sikorsky, being a flying boat, did not. There were many occasions when the *Phoenix* would manage to steam right in front of the Sikorsky as she was leaving the dock. The only thing that Captain Probert could do was shut down all four engines and hope that his ship would not collide with anything. You could see the steam rise from the cockpit whenever this happened.

The glass bottom boats would leave the steamer pier and head for the underwater seaweed gardens that teem with fish. The marine gardens are located in the small "Lover's Cove" next to Avalon bay. This area is a marine preserve where fishing is specifically prohibited. For over 100 years, the native fish in this cove have been fed by man. Originally, fish food was thrown from the glass bottom row boats. Later (in the 1940's - 50's) hard hat divers hand fed the fish each time a sightseeing boat entered the area. Two people in particular (in addition to the Harrison and Hernandez families), Al and Norma Hanson, popularized this added attraction while wearing Navy hard hat diving suits. The Hanson family (including son - Gary) also offered the main diving service in Avalon for such tasks as setting up floats, moorings, and retrieving large or valuable items dropped overboard by yachtsmen.

The Lover's Cove area immediately to the south of Avalon bay might witness the arrival of a couple of dock boys on an infrequent day off of work. Typically, dock boys received one day off per week. This was the day to do the things that were not possible during the other six days. For roommates, sleeping late received first priority, followed by dropping off six days worth of dirty Bermuda shorts, socks, and airline shirts at the Avalon Laundromat to clean (but not press). Socks were especially bad. Mixing salt water, sweat, and a few days worth of wearing, creates a very potent load for the nasal passages. Many possible romances were ruined because a dock boy didn't have time to go home after work to change socks before going out for the evening. After sleeping in, and depositing the week's laundry into the closest machine, you could head for the Pancake Cottage restaurant. There you would order (from Freddy Machado - perennial waiter) no less than two full "Country Breakfasts" apiece.

The standard Country Breakfast consisted of orange juice, coffee, toast, with your choice of ham, bacon or sausage, hash browns, and a stack of pancakes. Two of these big breakfasts for each dock boy helped to replace the calories burned during the rest of the week. After dining, you would return to the Laundromat to check on your wash and put it in the dryer. Because no one had the time (or interest) to separate colors, you sometimes wound up with multi-colored underwear.

With the chores part of the day nearly finished, you would head for the airline office to see how everyone was doing, and then visit the Avalon Fish Market to pick up some bait. Procuring a boat, fishing gear, some beer and the bait, you headed for the US Coast Guard mooring can to tie up. This mooring can was used by the Coast Guard when they brought their ocean-going cutter to the island. The mooring was located at the face of the bay right next to the undersea gardens. From there, we would cast our lines toward (but not in) the protected area in Lover's Cove where the glass bottom boats dwelled. The fish from this area were healthy indeed, because of the localized feeding for the boat tours. We were careful not to cast when Captain Harrison was in the vicinity. After catching enough fish to make dinner for four, we would head back to the pier, where we returned the skiff and fishing gear. We then began to search the beach for culinary assistance. It was now about mid-day and bathing beauties had begun to assemble on the beaches. We would search out among them those that could help us select the proper wine and salad fixings from Shaug Park's Island Grocery, and then properly prepare our catch. On the way home, we would retrieve our now dried (and stacked on the floor) uniforms from the Laundromat. Our day was almost complete.

Cross Channel Kayaker

Sometimes a little authority can go to your head and get you in trouble. One sunny summer day about mid-morning a small, open-topped kayak was paddled up to our seaplane floats by a little old man who had sunburned legs and a handkerchief (with a knot in each corner) tied to the top of his sunburned head. As he landed, the wake

Warner McIntyre takes tickets from passengers boarding Goose N323. This ship was one of two that had retractable pontoons and could carry up to 11 passengers. The glass bottom boat Phoenix *returns to the Steamer Pier.*

of a passing, slowly moving, shore boat nearly swamped his fragile craft.

All dock boys had been instructed by our Station Manager to keep our floats clear at all times—awaiting the arrival of our aircraft. We were constantly having to deal with pleasure craft drivers who wanted to "temporarily" tie up to send the wife to get some ice, fish bait, or what have you. As you can imagine—especially on a busy weekend—if any boat driver had seen our floats were available—we would have had a real traffic jam. In addition, we would have incurred the wrath of the Harbor Master—who wanted the mooring fees from these mariners, and the ire of the shore boat operators—who would lose revenue too.

So, as I placed a hand on the bow of the little old man's kayak, I recited my practiced line;

"*Please use the orange floats at the side of the pier for loading and unloading.*"

To which the little old man replied;

"But, I just paddled all the way from the mainland."

Oh, well, sure — this guy in his 70's or 80's had just paddled 26 miles more or less — with only a double-bladed oar, in an open (7' or 8') kayak across the open ocean on a summer Saturday morning. So I repeated my canned speech, and pushed the bow off in the direction of the City's orange float on the side of the pier.

About ten minutes later, I was pushing a cart load of luggage from an incoming flight down to the land end of the pier, when I immediately encountered a crowd near the ramp landing for the City float. About 200 people, the Mayor, the Catalina Islander newspaper reporter, and two LA County Sheriffs officers were all assembled at pier side. I asked one of the bystanders what was the occasion, to which he responded;

"Some elderly gentleman just paddled solo - across the channel from the mainland."

Just then, as I looked down at the City float, I saw the little old man and his kayak. He was gesticulating toward our airline floats and complaining about something to one of the greeting dignitaries. At this point, I hurried to deliver my cart of bags, as I didn't want to keep our passengers waiting.

Sandwiches

Here is the story of how I got married. One day, a traveling salesman spent the day making his rounds of Avalon and was waiting at our front counter for his return flight to the mainland. His line of goods was furnishing a new type of infrared fast food cooker, and then selling the food items to go with it. Many times the dock boys had rushed to work in the morning and hadn't had time for a well rounded breakfast including the four basic food groups. And, of course, sometimes the typical dock boy might not have been able to face a breakfast of any food group — until later in the day.

Our fast food choices on or near the pier were somewhat limited. There was the very popular donut shop, but it was a little too far up the street for the standard dock boy in a hurry. Restaurants were out of the question, but there were two options available right on the Pleasure Pier. One was the Avalon Fish Market. This place was wonderful. Fresh fish, crab, lobster, orange juice, milk—just about anything a dock boy could ask for. Many of us had a running charge account tab that we could run up—so we didn't have to worry about carrying cash. But this place was sometimes very busy, and you couldn't get an order in. Also, in the course of a week you could run up a very large tab—which you might have trouble covering on our minimum wage pay.

The other option on the pier was Eric's hamburger stand—which was also very busy. Eric's was owned and operated by Eric. Eric did not like dock boys—there was a genuine generation gap here. We were loud, fast, flip, and Eric was just the reverse. Eric's hamburgers were classic: you received a sesame seed bun, a patty, a thin slice of cheese, and either/or catsup and mustard and pickles. No lettuce or tomato. You could get onion—but we were probably going to try to get a date for that night —during our lunch time. Also, you could run up a big bill here too during the week—no tabs at Eric's because he knew that we were possibly shaky on payments.

So, the answer was obvious, make our own sandwiches. In no time I had signed the agreement with the salesman for the "free" cooker, and placed an order for a variety of pre-packaged sandwiches that were offered. Within the week, the sandwiches had arrived, and we had a thriving business operating out of the back of the airline office. The cost to the dock boy (only dock boys were served) for each sandwich was only a nickel over the gross cost of the "raw" material. These sandwiches were not the freshest, nor the best. We had names for some of them; "barf & burn" burritos was one that I remember with fondness. The extra nickel "profit" went into the dock boy fund (also deposited there were any tips that a dock boy might receive). Over the next several weeks, the dock boy fund swelled—and we just had to spend the money.

I know, I know, I am getting to the "how I got married" part next.

Party down the coast

Here's how the surplus cash in the dock boy fund was spent — we would throw a beach party. First, we would reserve a beach at a cove a few miles down the coast through the Santa Catalina Island Company. The Company controlled all island properties including Toyon Bay, the Girl Scout Camp at White's Landing, and other coves past Long Point where we would sometimes stage our extravaganzas. Then we would hire a shore boat to take the bulk of the party-goers to the cove after work. We would also pay to have a keg of beer flown from the mainland (the wing bins on 881 were the perfect size for such a task) to arrive just in time for the last flight to Avalon. We would then store the keg in the walk-in refrigerator at the fish market until the shore boat left for the beach party. Hot dogs, buns, marshmallows, all of the fixings for your standard evening on the beach were bought and paid for out of the dock boy funds.

Such fun under the stars was not exempt from danger. One night as we were singing songs around the campfire, noises were heard coming from the brush behind us. Upon investigation, we found that a pack of the infamous Catalina wild boar were digging up the area looking for food. These beasts are pugnacious to say the least. They are not the cute, smooth pink kind of pig — they truly are wild animals with scraggly hairs sticking up, nasty looking tusks, and much exuberant grunting as they forage. They scared most of the girls and some of the boys. However, several of the well lubricated college boys quickly drove the piglets off with boisterous shouting. Sometimes we would take sleeping bags for an overnight camp out. We had to be at work on the floats in the bay early in the morning. We would get up at dawn, load our boats and speed toward Avalon. I have beautiful memories of skimming along on water like glass toward the bay and the rising sun. One morning, I caught movement out of my peripheral vision coming up from behind on my left. Flying just inches above the glassy surface was a line of seven pelicans — with the leader driving his wings and the others all drafting behind. Magic. We could afford to do beach parties up to three times in a summer.

And now we will discuss how I fell in love and got married. It was during the preparation for one of these down-the-coast beach extravaganzas that I met my future wife—Janet. All day long, I had been busy with all of the organization and coordination for that evening's fest when I realized that I didn't have a date for the darned thing! So, as I was buying a soda pop at Eric's, I remembered this cute helper at the counter—and I asked her if she was going to the party that night. She responded *"what party?"* and the rest is history.

All of the fun and free enterprise that was produced by the dock boy sandwich sales came to a screeching halt one day. It seems that word had gotten out that the dock boys were not buying their sustenance from any member of the Chamber of Commerce, nor was their food dispensary being inspected by any official of any public health agency. We were promptly shut down by the powers that be. We ate the last of the sandwiches, returned the sandwich cooker to the salesman, and shut down operations. We kept on partying anyway.

Bruce the Barracuda

No question about it, we were the center of attention because our operation was located in the middle of Avalon Bay. Several factors combined to create this attention. The takeoff and landing operations of the beautiful aircraft in our fleet were flashy and just plain neat. Many islanders and lots of tourists rode on our ships, and knew who we were and what we did. We also had a crew of highly mobile uniformed "men about town" who (usually) moved quickly and were also seen at night. During the day, however, we were most visible. Two specific activities attracted attention—some desired, some not.

This was especially true when it came to diving off of the wing of the Sikorsky. There were times during the middle of the day when we were between flights—and there would be a lull of about an hour or so. This was the perfect time for many forces to come together—overheated dock boys, no inbound or outbound flights, an idle seaplane parked at the docks—all of these items led to diving off the wing of the flying boat.

Part IV — Adventures in Paradise

When tied up to the dock, all of the Sikorsky's aviation fuel was in the starboard wing, which meant that the port wing was up in the air high enough for dock boys to dive off and get some impressive splashes upon landing. We did solos, dual dives, group aerials, you name it and we tried it (at least once).

One other fun activity related to wing diving came about because there were many bikini-clad young women who would assemble on the pier above the seaplane docks to be entertained. An enterprising dock boy named Greg Harris dreamed up the following scheme in order to get closer to the numerous bathing beauties who would gather at the top of the pier to view the antics below. The plan worked this way; just after the departure of the 1:30 pm Goose flight to LGB, Greg would hold a "Bruce the Barracuda" feeding on the floats. Girls would be solicited on the beach during the morning (or during the prior evening) to view and hand feed a baby barracuda named "Bruce."

The story, as told by Greg, is that he had spotted this sick baby barracuda hanging around the floats one day and had proceeded to nurse it back to health. Now healthy, the fish would not leave his adopted parent and waited around the floats to be fed. For the daily feeding, Greg, and others, would hand out gate passes to a set number of young ladies, for a specific time. The prospective feeders were also instructed in advance to pick up some "Bruce food" (fish guts or squid chunks) from the adjacent fish market.

The girls would show up at their appointed time, with fish guts, their gate pass, and their bikinis. They would be escorted onto the floats—under the wing of the Sikorsky—and were told to jump up and down and call or whistle to alert Bruce. Greg, or one of his disciples, would yell at an opportune moment, *"there he is."* With great excitement, the girls would be told to put their food offering into the water and Bruce would eat out of their hand. Bruce never did, but all of the girls went swimming. There was a great deal of muttering as the girls returned to the beach, but none of them would report the truth. Rather, they would solicit new recruits for the next feeding. On a good day, there might be three or four Bruce feedings. Some people even brought their movie cameras to show the folks back home what they had observed during their summer vacation.

But there was trouble brewing in paradise. The Harbor Master also observed our activities.

One particular summer, the Harbor Master and all of his assistant Harbor Masters were made semi-official law enforcement officers. One night at a City Council meeting the entire Harbor Department had been deputized, and the following morning they all began wearing Los Angeles County Sheriff's badges.

In addition, new signs sprouted all along the pier which stated:

> NO DIVING
> Unlawful to enter water from pier or floats.
> ORD. No. 421
> Harbor Master - City of Avalon

I know precisely what these signs look like - because I still have mine.

We didn't much notice the new badges or signs but, sure enough, after one of the dock boys dove off of the wing, down onto the floats came the Harbor Master sporting his new badge, threatening arrest and who-knows-what-all if anybody tried that particular act again. Well, let me tell you, this put a real crimp in many of our extra curricular activities. Our response to his action brought to mind one of "Johnston's Rules of Life," to wit; *"For every attempt to control there is an equal and opposite attempt to circumvent those controls, and usually with greater ingenuity."*

The Harbor Master was a well meaning gentleman but he was more than a little impressed with his position. In addition, there was a prior history of friction going back 10 to 15 years between the Harbor Master and Dick Probert. To quote Probert from his essay on the subject, "The Harbor Master was one of three old cronies who had been in Avalon for over 30 years. They were all there during

Prohibition in this country and the operator of a speed boat... These three had lots of friends in town... Some of his cronies hatched up a plan to get rid of AAT."

During the second summer of AAT operations, the Harbor Master summoned the US Coast Guard Commander from Long Beach in an attempt to rid the bay of the airline. He called a meeting at his office with Dick Probert and the Coast Guard official to make a decision once and for all. While all observed the interplay of boats and planes from the top of the pier, a boat appeared with two ladies driving. It appeared to be out of control. The Harbor Master said that this was a perfect example of the dangers of mixing boats and planes in his harbor. Probert said that the whole incident looked as if it had been staged. The Commander said that the airline appeared to operating in a safe manner—and that they should be allowed to continue. What the Harbor Master did not know was that the Commander was a former Goose pilot for Coast Guard.

The Harbor Master was a short grumpy man, and he walked with a peculiar side to side motion belying a probable bad back. The dock boys' view was that he had another problem—he had a Napoleonic Complex. In order to mirror his unique personality, we had a dish at the fish market named in his honor—the "Harbor Master Cocktail." The real name of the cocktail is changed here to protect the innocent. This dish was made of equal parts shrimp and crab. At lunchtime, ordering a "Harbor Master Cocktail" would get you the correct item—no questions asked.

In response to the threats of arrest, we sent one of the dock boys down to one of Avalon's most important shops - the "Fun Shop" to purchase some badges for our own crew. We all immediately began wearing "Official Officer," "Junior G-Man," and "Secret Agent" badges as part of our everyday uniforms. Then, we remembered a damaged and abandoned rowboat - about 6' in length that resided in a dark corner of the bay. It was added forthwith to our fleet of water craft to be used—usually by several dock boys at a time—whenever we wanted to cool off or thumb our noses at old "wiggle-waggle" as

Sikorsky co-pilot George Briggs, Udo Waldman, and Bob Frost maneuver our very unstable skiff just before it capsized—in clear view of the Harbor Masters' office.

we sometimes called him. We became quite adept at capsizing this holy skiff in plain view of the ever-watchful eye of "his honor."

In addition to barracuda, other sea fauna played a role in dock boy adventures. A baby seal showed up one day sitting on one of the mooring floats that were used to tie up the Gooses. We took the Woody boat out to the float to investigate. Up close, this little fellow looked terrible. He had gunk all over his nose and he was coughing so loudly that we could hear him from our seaplane floats 50 yards away. We took our problem to one of the most precious resources a dock boy could have—Leo's Pharmacy. Located on the front street of the bay, Leo's was run by Leo Zager and his wife Ethel.

Leo's was extremely useful to a dock boy in distress. Many times, a dock boy would come down with some (hopefully minor) ailment— but there was no point in seeing the doctor. First, we couldn't afford to pay for the medical treatment. Second, the medical services situation in Avalon consisted of one doctor who was viewed with some suspicion by the locals. In times of medical need, we would turn instead to Leo. He could diagnose with the best of them, and he would then sell us — or many times give us free samples of — the best medicine for whatever ailed us. I would bet that some of the medicine he dispensed to us probably needed a prescription — I am not sure how he handled this. For the sick baby seal, Leo recognized an upper respiratory infection when he heard one. So he gave us some pills and some instructions. We put the proper amount of pills in the proper amount of fish scraps from the fish market and promptly hand fed the remedy to the seal pup. During the treatment the baby seal stayed on the mooring float for a couple of days. He became very tame. After a couple of days, he migrated to the Joe's Rent-a-Boat floats, closer to the beach. Even though the medication was no longer needed, the dock crew at Joe's continued to feed and pay attention to the seal. The seal knew a good thing when he saw it and hung around for several more days before returning to the sea. Leo had saved another of Mother Nature's creatures.

The Avalon Fish Market played a very important part in the lives of the airline dock boys. It provided bait for fishing on days off, food for Bruce, storage for kegs of beer waiting for that night's soiree, and food and drink to keep the undernourished dock boy from starvation. The owners of the fish market liked the dock boys — we were all regular customers and we were neighbors on the end of the pier. So, it was no surprise when owner Rose "Rosy" Cadman offered to make a big shark scallopine dinner for all of the airline crew. One night, she showed up right after work, plunked down a huge stainless steel pot filled to the brim with her delicious concoction. We all ate several plates-full and enjoyed it thoroughly. It wasn't until later that night that we realized what she had done to us. We were in the Avalon High School gymnasium, playing a basketball game against the team that her son was on, when we really started to feel the full effects of our overindulgence in her tasty dish.

The fish market was sometimes the starting point for a relaxing evening of "sharkin." Some fish parts or "chum" would be obtained to take in the Woody boat after dark. Other ingredients for the evening included; a couple of dock boys, a lantern, the chum, and Jerry

Williams with his machete. Once outside the harbor, the chum and the lantern were sure to bring a shark at which time Jerry would take a whack at him with his knife. One memorable trip occurred when Jerry missed the shark and put a hole in the side of the Woody boat. Occasionally, a shark would be caught and sold to the fish market.

Keeping Busy

During the quiet parts of the normal work day at the seaplane base, a number of diversions were employed to break the tedium. Initiating new dock boys was always a crowd pleaser. Most new candidates would apply for the job of dock boy during the winter or spring and then try out for the position during spring break week. In late spring, we would start getting phone calls in the office from residents who lived on the hillsides around the bay, asking when the "new guys" were coming. Remember that this is a small town, on an island—with limited diversions for year-round residents.

One popular attraction the hillside residents enjoyed was when uninitiated dock boys were used in the role of the "FAA Flagman." To fully grasp this duty, you need to know that our airline had a competitor. Our competition flew from San Pedro, on the mainland, to Pebbly Beach about one mile down the coast from the bay. Pebbly Beach has a paved amphibian ramp that was built in 1959 and it was used by Catalina Channel Airlines, who also flew Grumman Gooses in their operations.

A typical "Flagman" episode was comprised of the following sequence of events. Dock boys (including the uninitiated) would be standing around the office during a dead time between flights. Suddenly, one of the perpetrators would look at the teletype and say *"there's an FAA inspector on the next flight!"* At once, we would latch onto the new guy, and race him down the ramp to one of the boats, stopping first at the equipment locker (called the coffin), to grab a broomstick with a red rag stapled to it. Jumping in the boat and rapidly casting off, we would begin to tell the importance of the flagman position to the candidate.

Part IV — Adventures in Paradise

The story went that the FAA was worried about the safety exposure with Gooses coming from Pebbly Beach (or the isthmus) and flying across the face of the bay. If one of our Gooses was arriving or departing at that time, there could be a tragedy. Therefore, it was the duty of the flagman to position himself on top of the US Coast Guard mooring can. Remember, that this same one was used for tying up the Coast Guard cutter and for dock boy fishing on boy days off. This metal ball was about four feet in diameter, located about 250 yards from shore, covered with seagull leavings, and topped with a large welded ring with a rope hawser attached.

During the boat trip out to the mooring can, the flagman was instructed to wave the flag rapidly when there was no other air traffic. That way, our pilot (and the FAA inspector) could see that it was safe to takeoff or land. The moment of truth came as we approached the mooring can—usually bobbing up and down wildly in the swells—to see if he was buying the safety plan. In seven years, I cannot remember any refusal to serve in the interest of saving lives. Of course, the pilots were advised by radio that there was a "flagman" on duty for their arrival. Usually, the pilot would land, taxi over, allowing the incoming passengers to get a close look, and then put the tail of the Goose toward the new guy on the mooring and then rev the engines slightly. Take offs were even more exciting for the flagman recruit. Full power from both engines can create a substantial amount of thrust (wind, water, etc.).

One dock boy in particular helped satisfy our FAA requirements. He was from the Long Beach harbor base—the overnight home of the Sikorsky. This particular day, he was the designated bowman for the flying boat. On busy days, the bowman would ride on the Sikorsky for several consecutive round trips as a member of the crew. His duties were to help load and unload luggage in the cavernous bow compartments, and to manage the bow line hookup when docking. Usually, the bowman was a member of the dock crew from the Long Beach harbor. Occasionally, an Avalon dock boy would serve the role.

I have wonderful memories of spending a hectic 10 to 15 minutes of offloading and then loading on baggage of all kinds followed by an invigorating 10 to 15 minute ride as a crew member. Although not FAA legal, if you made the channel transit riding in the bow, you could stick your head out of the bow hatch located at the very nose of the ship. This hatch was usually left open during the short summer flights, allowing for some ventilation through the length of the ship. What an excellent vantage point! It was very refreshing and you could feel the power and speed of this beautiful flying boat with your face riding at the very front of the slipstream. Best of all, Captain Probert could not see you "cooling it" because you and the hatch were below his forward line of vision.

Now, back to our particular Long Beach harbor dock boy. After docking in Avalon and pitching the luggage out of the flying boat's bow, this dock boy's regular routine would be to immediately amble down the pier and take a break—or go to lunch. Never mind that the rest of us were unloading freight from the wing bins on the Sikorsky, unloading and loading one or two Gooses at the end of the floats, or pushing carts up the steep ramp. Totally ignoring any other tasks, off he would go. One day we caught him right at the top of the ramp as he tried to exit, and employed him as the FAA flagman. Out he went to the Coast Guard mooring can. And then we forgot about him. He wasn't one of our regular crew, so we didn't really miss him not being around. About three hours later, we recognized our mistake, but he was not to be found. We used the binoculars, we sent out both boats to look, but no flagman. Finally, he showed up in time for the Sikorsky to depart (at 4:00 pm). He was dry. Someone asked him how he got back to shore. He said that he swam to Casino Point and then walked back. I don't remember if we ever saw him again after that day.

Our airline owner, chief pilot, and captain of the Sikorsky—Dick Probert had many employees. He really didn't like to see them being non-productive. Many times, he would arrive in Avalon on the last flight of the morning, and on his way to lunch, he would issue instructions to the Station Manager for various tasks to be carried out during his absence. One of his favorites was for the dock boys to clean and polish the Pitot tube. This tube is used on aircraft as a steady source of outside air which is fed to the pressure gauges on the instrument panel. Without it, altitude and air speed indications would not be accurate. Mounted on the bow of the Sikorsky, this air intake is a little over one foot high with two streamlined tubes about 6 inches long jutting like arrows into the airflow. It is made of copper and subject to instant corrosion by salt water and weather. It was always turning green. Probert's instructions to the Station Manager were, once again, *"have them clean it."* These instructions were relayed to me. This time, I decided that we needed some chemical assistance. Presenting my difficulty to the proprietor of the Avalon Paint Shop, I was handed a pint of a new coating on the market, "Varathane."

This was in the good old days, before environmental awareness about paints and solvents, so this was the real stuff. After carefully steel-wooling the Pitot tube, we applied this magic coating and it worked like a charm. From that time on, Captain Probert would check the Pitot tube before leaving for lunch and gently shake his head as he walked off the floats.

Nearly everyone knows about the mystery of places such as the "Bermuda Triangle" and other locations on earth where unexplained phenomena occur. Catalina Air Lines had one such place of its own — right on the Pleasure Pier. The main operations office was at the water end of the pier — but there was also a satellite office at the land end of the pier. This location was generally used for ticket sales, reservations, luggage checking, and temporary storage. It was a one person office. People went a little crazy in there. Perhaps not everyone who worked there became afflicted, but most of them did. While working in this office, at least four guys "went bazooney" as the dock boys used to say. The symptoms went like this: We would get strange responses over the hot line phone that ran between the two offices. The lonesome guy would issue semi-coherent statements, make incomplete calls to the main office, or not answer questions in an understandable manner. Reservation requests many times did not make sense.

The author in uniform with Bonnie Gill in front of the land end office in 1963.

This office was a hub of activity. It was located in a strategic spot where all of the traffic on the main street, the pier, the beach, and to and from the woman's restroom passed by. There were many distractions. The front counter was at just the right height for girls wearing swimsuits to rest their chests on. People came at you from all directions—asking questions, checking luggage—certainly, the stimulation factor was high. The final act for each of the four manifested itself in outward aggression. They all threw items from the office windows or door. Golf clubs, luggage, freight, paperwork, baggage tags, a box of oranges (one at a time), and brochures all were hurled street-ward when each of these over-stressed ticket agents reached the breaking point. The only agents who seemed to maintain their sanity closed all of the windows except the front counter, and locked the door to keep all of the action in front of them. We never did figure it out.

Part IV — Adventures in Paradise

The Beatle Hoax

During the summer of 1965, the four members of the British group *The Beatles* were the hottest attraction in the music world. They were touring the United States that summer and had received a tumultuous welcome at every city they visited. They had also again appeared on one of the most watched TV shows—The Ed Sullivan variety hour. Things were at a fever pitch. Thousands of fans had mobbed the airports, hotels, and show venues every time the shaggy-hired group appeared. Young girls screamed and swooned.

The "Fab Four" was scheduled to appear this particular weekend in August for a concert at the Hollywood Bowl on the mainland. That quiet Saturday morning about 10:30, two teenage girls in bikinis were standing at the pier rail looking down into the green/gold water below. They were only about 20 feet from the front counter of the airline office. A voice from our office spoke:

"Boy, it sure will be crowded around here when the Beatles get here today."

The two young ladies looked at one another, back down at the water, and then back at one another. They turned together and approached the counter.

One asked: *"What time are the Beatles coming in today?"*
Office: *"Well, let me check with the mainland office."*

After typing the current weather conditions in Avalon Bay on the teletype, and waiting for a response, (which was "So what?"), the dock boy said:

"They don't show any Beatles coming today, but they do show a party of four under the name of Star on the 4:00 pm flight today."

It should be noted for the young reader or the uninformed that the Beatles drummer was named Ringo Starr, and was known to probably every teenager alive at that time.

"Oh goody, thank you very much!"

And off they ran toward the beach.

A very short time later, more teenagers began showing up at the front counter with the same query. This exchange repeated itself with larger numbers of teenagers and greater frequency as the day progressed. By afternoon, the airline office had received calls from the Mayor's office—wanting to present the key to the City, the Los Angeles County Sheriff's Office—wanting to cordon off the pier for security, the Catalina Islander newspaper office—wanting an interview, and the Catalina Airport-in-the-Sky—wondering if the Beatles were supposed to arrive there. Needless to say, by 3:00 pm, the entire pier from the beach all the way to the water end was packed with thousands of people—you couldn't even walk, let alone get a baggage cart through the throng. Every Rent-a-boat was out circling in the bay, pleasure craft of all types and sizes were under way so they could see through the windows of any aircraft approaching the docks. The airline office phones were ringing constantly. Clearly, this was a joke that had gotten out of control.

At this point, one of the dock boys asked if he should have a little fun. He wanted to go down to the Avalon Fun Shop, buy four wigs (remember that the Beatles were known for their long hair), and get his guitar. His "plan" was to enter the bow hatch of the Sikorsky with three other dock boys, don the wigs and exit from the passenger door at the rear of the ship. I told him "no" and therefore, that day, I figure that I saved at least four lives.

Winter in Avalon

Winter on Catalina Island is usually peaceful. The influx of tourists dwindles as schools go back in session and the temperature starts to cool off. By October the island is idyllic with moderate weather, few tourists, and generally relaxed schedules for the remaining year-round citizens. This is a chance to catch up on chores and projects. Some businesses close down completely until spring. However, those who operate on or near the water have some extra precautions that must be taken—to protect from the ravages of the sea in winter.

Part IV — Adventures in Paradise

For the seaplane base operation in Avalon Bay, several changes had to be made every fall. Once the air passenger traffic to the island began to fall off, it was not economically feasible to continue the Sikorsky flying boat schedule. 881 would then be hauled up on the mainland for routine maintenance and storage until the following spring weather had improved the passenger demand. This meant that the full docking float configuration was no longer needed. In addition, winter storms could destroy these floats easily because they projected directly out toward the face of the bay with open sea exposure. The Pleasure Pier amphibian float configuration for the winter consisted of one ramp and two small floats that projected from the side of the pier rather than the end. Usually these floats could stay in place because they were relatively sheltered from the sea, however, after the last flight of the day, the ramp would be lifted onto the pier for the night. This was accomplished with a cable and a hoist that was attached to the pier.

Actually, there were three different levels of precaution that could be taken depending on the weather forecast for overnight and the amount of risk that the Station Manager was willing to take. You could lift the ramp only. This was easy to do and only added about five minutes to the start and end of the work day. The second level of caution called for lifting the ramp and removing the floats from their securing cables next to the pier and towing them out to the mooring floats that were normally used to temporarily "park" Grumman Gooses. The floats could ride out most swells from this location. This involved unhooking the floats from their cables, attaching the floats — one at a time — to the Woody boat, and then towing them out to the moorings. This procedure added about 20 or 30 minutes to both ends of the work day. In addition to having to get up earlier, this was extra hard work that involved cold, wet fingers, shoes, and clothes. Level two caution was reserved for weather predictions of moderate storms.

The third (and ultimate) level of precaution meant pulling everything from the bay. When gale warnings with high winds and rough seas were forecast, we would use the small hoist to lift the ramp and store it, and also use the BIG hoist to raise both floats onto the top of the pier. These floats were very heavy—the main float was 50 feet long. This operation was the equivalent of lifting a small house, and the procedure was made more difficult by a couple of other factors. At the end of the day it was starting to get dark, and the wind preceding the storm was usually blowing hard. For these reasons, we would sometimes gamble and leave the floats in. Besides, we reasoned, the weather usually turns out better than the forecast. I remember one night—about 2:00 a.m.—awakening to the sound of wind howling through the attic vents over my bedroom. I quickly called some cohorts, woke them up too, and went down to pull the floats from the dark, cold, storm-ravaged bay. Those were the good old days.

The storm that causes the most concern in Avalon bay is so feared that it has a name—it is called a "Northeaster." Some other parts of the world also have significant local winds that have names. They are colorful names, pretty enough to name boats after, like Sirocco and Mistral. In Avalon, the "Nor'easter" is caused by a winter high pressure area that blows hot, high velocity winds off of the desert directly into the face of the bay from a north easterly direction. These hot blasts from the desert are also called "Santa Anas" One Northeaster still lives vividly in my memory.

Upon hearing the forecast, we pulled the floats and had begun to wait it out. The wind had started to blow early in the evening and we all went to the harbor to watch the impending storm as it gathered in intensity. All boats in the harbor had been moved to the most sheltered moorings. Other operators in the bay had pulled their own floats including the fuel dock, the shore boats, and the Tuna Club, etc. Everything that could be secured was cinched down tight. The evening was clear—all the clouds were blown hundreds of miles to the southwest, and even though it was winter, it was warm from the desert winds. After about two hours of rising wind and sea, some of the boats that were the furthest out in the bay broke loose from their moorings. These boats then smashed into those that were behind them.

One sailboat had broken loose and was sitting sideways against the seawall next to the Steamer Pier. It had been abandoned hastily and it still had the cabin lights on and her deck chairs set up out in the open cockpit. This beautiful ship was banging against the seawall and each time it hit, the bronze ships bell clanged alarmingly—its fate was certain. By midnight, the waves were so high that the windows in our airline office that faced the sea were broken out. The Station Manager asked if I would sleep in the unsecured office overnight. I jumped at the chance to be a part of the excitement. What a mistake. I had to scrape the broken glass and then most of the seawater from the top of the office desk in order to sleep on it. The wind howled and the waves crashed under and over the pier all night.

In the morning, I surveyed the scene. In the office all paper goods were ruined, the windows facing the bay were gone, the floor was covered with debris and saltwater, and the teletype had fried itself. The Station Manager showed up and I helped him man the telephones for a couple of hours to make sure that the flights were operating in and out of the Airport-In-The-Sky. Finally, since there was nothing a looter would want, the Station Manager figured that he could cover things so he sent me to go get cleaned up and get something to eat. The bay was a disaster area, and here at least, I don't exaggerate.

The area around the large hoist on the Pleasure Pier was covered with engines that had been salvaged and lifted from the bay. These engines no longer had boats to go with them—there must have been three dozen in-boards engines and outboards—of all sizes. All of the lumber, fiberglass, rubber, and anything else that had once made up the missing boats was now jammed underneath the two piers. Piles of debris that had once been someone's ocean going pleasure craft had been reduced to rubble by the pounding of the overnight sea. The beautiful sailboat whose bell had been clanging so forlornly the night before was no more. All that was left—sitting at the same spot along the seawall—was its lonely engine left high on the rocks.

It would ultimately take days to remove all of the items that the storm had left and, sadly, among the remains of boats there had been one fatality. By mid-morning, the TV news crews arrived from the mainland to cover the disaster. Who do you think they interviewed for the real story about the storm and its effects? The Harbor Master riding the storm tossed waves looking for survivors? The undersea divers retrieving lost articles? The various rescue workers performing all manner of difficult and dangerous work? No, it was actress June Lockhart, who had spent the night in a hotel. She was taking a little time off from a TV series that she was starring in at that time and was visiting the island. Groggy from my overnight surveillance duties, I was in the Crescent Café getting a cup of coffee when I noticed the TV crew interviewing her at her table. I also remember that she was immaculately made up and wearing dry clothes.

Christmas time for the airline crew in Avalon was a mixture of joy and sadness. Islanders would be traveling "over town" to see friends and relatives, or they would be welcoming those who were coming to Avalon for the holidays. Most of the time, the Avalon airline crew was made up of single men who had no relatives on the island and could not leave the island because they had to work during the busy holiday travel time. In order to get into the spirit of the season, we decided that we needed a tree. Christmas trees are very expensive in Southern California. They don't grow there; they have to be imported from up north and it is a sellers market. However, near the city dump on a hill east of Avalon there is a stand of Norfolk Pines.

One night a week or two before Christmas, a couple of us drove the Catalina Air Lines van up to the dump to requisition a tree for the airline office. We hunted, selected, cut and transported the small tree down to the office on the pier, figuring to decorate it the next day. The next morning—remember that no one has traveled to or from the island over night—the very first teletype message received from the Long Beach Airport office was from the Vice-President of the airline. He wanted to know who had been driving the airline van near the dump the night before. What a small town! Some islander, who lives on the road to the dump no doubt, at the crack of dawn had called the mainland to report suspicious use of airline property. Anyway, the tree was finally decorated and looked beautiful. We then decided to see if we could diplomatically solicit some courtesy gifts for the good old airline crew. Each of us brought an empty liquor bottle to the office. There, we filled them with water, sealed and carefully wrapped them and put pretty bows on where appropriate. We placed them around the tree that sat in the front window and then attached gift tags with large block letters. Some sample tags read "To the Airline Gang - Hope You Enjoy," and "Cheers - from the Joneses." We actually got one or two more to add to our starter bottle collection.

The Airport-in-the-Sky

When the ocean in and around Avalon became too rough for aircraft takeoffs and landings, we would send the amphibians to SXC—better known as "the hill." This sounds simple—but it was not. The arriving Goose pilot would not know for sure if he could safely land on or near the bay until he had flown across the channel and taken a look. There were a few times when we could tell from our vantage point on the pier that there was no chance of landing, in which

Justin Dart flew the first (authorized) land plane to Catalina. He was a friend of Philip Wrigley and landed his Lockheed near Wrigley's ranch in the interior.

case we simply sent the first outbound passengers in a van to the hill. Most of the time, however, it was a 50-50 proposition as to whether the Goose would land on the bay or at the hill. On those occasions, we would cheat and send the van to a point about 15 minutes away from the bay. This is called "the summit," and it is about one-half way between the bay and the hill. It also had a small, hand-crank telephone in a box nailed to a eucalyptus tree next to the road. It should be remembered that in the 1960's the island telephone system consisted of mostly three digit phone numbers and employed real, live telephone operators who lived on the island. The telephones had no dials. To place a call from your home or office phone all you had to do was lift the receiver and, when the operator said "operator," you gave her the number that you wanted to call.

Before SXC was open to the public, landings were sometimes hazardous.

Part IV — Adventures in Paradise 183

The van driver would wait by the phone at the summit—I think the complete telephone number was 109-J or something like that—until he was called and told where the Goose pilot was landing. If the pilot had made the bay, the van driver would go back down to Avalon and off-load the passengers at the end of the pier. If the Goose landed at the hill, the van continued on to SXC where passengers would be exchanged.

United Air Lines Mainliner — arriving at Catalina's Airport in the sky.

There was no airport on the island before SXC construction was begun in the late 1930's. Attempts at earlier landings had various results. In 1929, a pilot from Glendale, California made a non-approved landing on the Catalina golf course—I wonder what the golfers thought about this. In 1935, Philip K. Wrigley's friend Justin Dart of Dart Industries—a major player in business and politics throughout the 20th century—landed his twin-engine airplane on the island. This was accomplished on a dusty road near the Wrigley ranch—El Rancho Escondido—in the interior of the island.

Many pilots tried to land in open fields and many crashes resulted. Five years later, in 1940, construction was begun on the Airport-in-the-Sky. This was a major project before the days of federal funding and the islanders got behind the effort. Surveys were made—which included pack mule camp outs—with measuring equipment to find the best location with regards to wind and weather.

Finally, three small peaks were bulldozed together—filling in between—to create the 3,100 foot long runway. Island resident Hugh Smith used a bulldozer to blade the three peaks smooth. His son Bud Smith later became a pilot for United Air Lines flying a DC-3 and landing on the field his father had helped to construct. When the airport was finished, two problems were encountered. First, the middle peak was formed from harder rock that the two outside peaks. The result is a runway that has a high point in the middle. With a drop off at each end and a high point in the middle, the "Airport in the Sky" is a challenge to pilots who are used to large flat runways. The second problem occurred after the three peaks were flattened. This change in topography also changed the local micro-climate resulting in occasional cloud formation over the runway. The result is one very interesting airport.

When World War II began, the military took over the partially completed airstrip. The military used the airstrip for flight training off and on during the war and, at different times, it was rendered unusable by placing a variety of obstacles across the runway. Telephone poles, barbed wire, and scrap metal were used. With the war finally over, the Santa Catalina Island Company (Wrigley) took over the operation of the landing strip. They constructed an airport terminal building in the same Mediterranean style as many other island buildings—including the accents using Catalina tile. They also moved the old hanger up from Hamilton Beach to the hill, and improved the old stagecoach access road from Avalon to the airport.

The old hanger was expanded to accommodate the DC-3 that Wrigley owned and kept on the island.

After the war, the airport was opened for commercial use and finally to the public in the late 1950's. Since the 1970's the airport has been owned and operated by the Santa Catalina Island Conservancy. It offers no fuel, oil, or parts but it offers an outstanding venue for access to the magic of the island. One other feature unique to SXC was—before fencing solved it—the buffalo problem. The island herd used to like the warmth of the runway and would frequently lay down on the pavement to rest. Sometimes, before a flight arrived at the hill, we had to run the airline van up and down the runway to chase the animals off. The US weather bureau personnel stationed at SXC also had a tough time keeping their landscaping from being destroyed by these bison in paradise.

KBIG

In the 1800's, homing pigeons were sometimes used by Catalina Island residents to send messages between the island and the mainland. In 1902, the first wireless telegraph station in the world was constructed in Avalon. By 1921, the first radio station began broadcasting from Avalon featuring —mainly—a program extolling the beauty and virtues of Santa Catalina. During World War II, the U.S. Army Signal Corps installed listening posts on the island because of its strategic location for intercepting and transmitting radio messages. In 1952, radio station KBIG began broadcasting from a hilltop site at Renton Pass on the road to the SXC. Because of the elevated location and transmission power, the station easily reached all of the Los Angeles Basin. To help advertise the station, one of their announcers, Carl Bailey, used to meet the steamer occasionally—especially if there were any dignitaries aboard. He was easy to spot waiting on the steamer pier because he was at least 6'6" and he customarily wore a jacket that said "I'm Big on KBIG" on the back. In the 1960's, one daily feature of KBIG was to broadcast the weather report both from Avalon Bay and, for boaters in the summertime, the wind and water conditions in the middle of the San Pedro Channel.

For example, the 10:00 am weather report was made up of two different pre-recorded reports. First, the radio station engineer would call the Catalina Air Lines office at the water end of the Pleasure Pier and record the report from the bay. Normally, the assistant in the office (usually Warner McIntire) would read from a script - filling in the blanks with the current temperature, barometric pressure, etc.

A typical bay report sounded like the following:

> *"Good morning, this is Warner McIntire reporting direct from the Pleasure Pier in Avalon bay. The current temperature in Avalon bay is 76 degrees, visibility is 3 miles, the wind is from the northeast at 4 miles per hour, and the barometric pressure is 30.07. This has been Warner McIntire for Catalina Air Lines reporting to you direct from beautiful Avalon bay."*

The pilot report from mid-channel was accomplished by transmitting an aircraft pilot report from the cockpit to the KBIG hilltop radio station using the normal aircraft radio. The radio station engineer would use an aircraft transceiver to call to any of the Catalina Air Lines ships that might be in mid-channel. He would then tape record the pilot's report (who would read from a script - filling in the current conditions - just like the bay report).

A typical pilot report sounded something like this:

> *"Good morning, this is Captain Warren Stoner in charge of Catalina Air Lines flight #19 reporting to you from mid-channel. Visibility is limited by fog. The wind conditions in mid-channel are from the north at 8 miles per hour, and the swells are from the west at about 2 to 3 feet. This has been Catalina Air Line's Captain Warren Stoner reporting to you from mid-channel."*

One very foggy summer morning, the KBIG station engineer called to record the usual Avalon Bay report. Warner McIntire did his normal task and was about to hang up the phone when the engineer asked why he hadn't been able to contact any CAL pilots for the mid-channel report. At this time, no aircraft had taken off because of an unusually dense and persistent fog. The engineer was stumped as to what to do for his pilot report - until we came up with a remedy.

In the airline office on the pier, we positioned Warner McIntire in between two dock boys who were in the office at the time. Since no aircraft were flying, dock boys had nothing to do except hang out in the office and drink orange juice or coffee. We then had Warner read from the pilot script—filling in what we knew the conditions usually were in mid-channel on a foggy day. A dock boy on either side of Warner made rhythmic droning sounds like the twin radials of the Grumman Goose. This sound was rendered especially effective by the proper cupping and un-cupping of the hands in front of the mouth to mimic the slightly out-of-synch rpm of the Goose propellers.

The engineer thanked us for the recording and hurried to prepare his tape for playback at the proper time. When the KBIG weather reports played that day—right on time at 10:00, Captain Warren Stoner was sitting in his MG convertible in the left turn lane, waiting to turn into the Long Beach airport to begin his flying day. It was still pretty foggy, but he knew that it would lift soon and he wanted to be ready for his first flight out—there would be some catching up to do with the backlog of unmade flights. As he listened to his car radio, the Avalon bay report sounded fine. But when he heard the in-flight report, he was extremely concerned that; (1) he had missed his responsibility for taking the first flight out, or (2) someone was impersonating him by flying one of the CAL Gooses. He was quite relieved upon his arrival that morning in Avalon to learn just how "his" weather report had been accomplished.

Another member of the Stoner family was involved in an island occurrence. One summer in the mid-1960's Warren's son Chuck—born in Hemet in 1943—was working as a dock boy at the Long Beach harbor seaplane base. On one of his days off, he took the Sikorsky to Avalon for the day. He enjoyed his time off in Avalon visiting with friends, as he had attended Avalon High School in the late 1950's when his dad had been Station Manager for Avalon Air. At the end of the day, he went to the Catalina Air Lines office at the end of the Pleasure Pier to check in for his return flight to the mainland, only to be told he had been "bumped"—which is airline lingo for losing your seat reservation to someone else. This was probably an intentional move on the part of the Avalon station personnel who knew two things: One, there was a very important league basketball game for the Catalina Air Lines team in the high school gym that night; and two, Chuck was a very good athlete.

After the last flight for the night departed, Chuck's impromptu addition to the team was greeted warmly by the Avalon dock boys—his nickname was "Stone Chucker" courtesy of fellow dock boy Dave Turner. He then went to the gym with the rest of the team and began to warm up for the game. During warmups, a taxi cab driver came to the door of the gym and began to holler Chuck's name. Chuck went over to talk with the driver who told him that he was to accompany him on a ride to the Airport where a plane would pick him up for his return trip to the mainland.

How had the cab driver been summoned, you ask? When the Long Beach harbor Station Manager John Chilcote saw that Chuck had not returned from the island, he was quite concerned. John knew that Chuck was needed the next morning to help prepare the Sikorsky flying boat for the day's flying. Always in danger of not having enough personnel to begin the day, John had previously impressed upon all of his dock boys that they would be fired if they did not show up for work in the morning.

John immediately called Chuck's mother, Alice Stoner, to express his concern. She then called the Proberts to see if there was anything they could do to help. Dick Probert called the Avalon Cab Company, and then Dick went to the Long Beach airport, took off in his personal plane (a two seat Luscome) and flew to the Catalina Airport that night to meet the taxi and pick up Chuck for the flight back to Long Beach.

The Luscome, a classic small plane, was not really equipped for either night or instrument flying. The instrument lighting consisted of a flashlight taped to a swivel on the cabin roof, and there were no radios installed in the ship. This would not have been a problem, except that the Long Beach airport was fogged in upon their return. Probert had to fly the Luscome out into the San Fernando Valley about 20 air miles north of Los Angeles to land at an airport where the fog was not as bad. After landing safely, Dick called his wife Nancy, who drove from Long Beach out to the Valley and the three of them drove to the Long Beach harbor to drop Chuck at the seaplane base. By this time—it was about 3:00 a.m.—they decided that they would leave Chuck—with a blanket from the trunk of the car—at the airline office so that he wouldn't be late for work.

The Proberts left Chuck with the blanket and some instructions: in the morning, before the Station Manager arrived, he should take himself and his blanket down to the dock where the Station Manager could find him. Upon discovery, Chuck was to say that he had swum back.

Tricksters

◆ Working for the airline we were surrounded by jokesters. Pilots, station personnel, dock boys—all were fertile sources for wit. Some was subtle, much was not. Dick Probert owned a brand new 1965 VW Squareback that he bragged about—especially the gas mileage that the salesman had promised him when he bought it. The crew at the Long Beach harbor seaplane base decided to add a small amount of gas to the tank every day while Dick was gone flying the Sikorsky. For weeks, Dick extolled the virtues of his new car and its performance. Then Dick took the car in to the dealer for its scheduled checkup. After Dick returned from the dealer with the VW, the crew at the seaplane base began to syphon off a quart or two of gas each day—which resulted in the gas mileage plummeting. Very perturbed, Dick took the car back to the dealer where he proceeded to discuss with them their tune up procedures.

◆ The Avalon Air Transport Station Manager in Avalon in the early 1960's was Anthony "Tony" Guion. In order to be the Station Manager, he had to take and pass a very rigorous test that the FAA required — the weather observer's license exam. Before the first flight from the mainland in the morning could depart, the FAA observer (Tony) had to issue a report by teletype stating the cloud cover height, visibility, winds, water conditions, and the current barometric pressure. Avalon weather had to be above the minimum FAA limits for a commercial plane to land. In the case of Catalina Air Lines, these minimums were a 500' ceiling and 1 mile forward visibility.

From the seaplane base on the pier it was very handy to know the elevation for various points around the bay. This could greatly assist weather conditions reporting without having to go to the trouble of sending up a weather balloon. Airline owner and chief pilot Dick Probert — always wanting to fly at the earliest opportunity — had helped Tony by giving him some of the elevations around the bay — particularly for Mt. Ada, where the Wrigley Mansion sat.

Tony was proud to hold his challenging position in the community and to represent the air line at various civic functions in Avalon. One day he was invited to a gathering at the Wrigley mansion, located on Mt. Ada overlooking Avalon bay. Tony was circulating among the crowd of dignitaries and exchanging pleasantries when he struck up a conversation with Malcom Renton — the head of the Santa Catalina Island Company. Tony commented on the beautiful view from the veranda at 500' above sea level. Whereby, Malcom politely informed Tony that the real height was 387' and that he might want to check his source of information.

◆ Located on the pier in the middle of the bay, the air line operation was a focal point for tourists. They regularly approached the office with all kinds of questions. Following are some examples:

Is this island completely surrounded by water?

Is this island part of Disneyland?

Where is the bridge?

What time does the fog lift?

Can I eat my lunch in the Undersea Gardens?

One tourist was describing the geography of the island to some of his friends. Regarding the Catalina isthmus, he said: *"It is the only place where you can see the Atlantic and the Pacific oceans at the same time."*

◆ Misinformation seemed to abound near the office. Sometimes there would be a trash fire burning at the island dump just over the hill from the bay and tourists would come out to our office on the pier and ask *"What is that smoke east of Avalon?"* To which we would reply; *"That is the island's only active volcano—"Mt. Garbagio."* They would leave nodding their heads knowingly.

One interesting story about the town dump: Avalon had a trash truck driver by the name of Guy Pullen. He would collect the trash and take it to "Mt. Garbagio" each week. While there, he saw many things that islanders had discarded and felt that many of those items had not outlived their usefulness. He began to collect items, large and small. Then he began to make things from wire, bedsprings, and hub caps. Soon he became a successful artist, making a living selling his unique art work designs.

◆ The town of Avalon is a great place for children. Walking is the main mode of transport and children can usually roam freely. They were frequent visitors to the air line office. Sometimes they became pests. On such occasions we would ask them to do us a favor—usually to go get us some item related to airplane safety. These willing couriers would launch off on errands to pick up such items as "bulkhead retainer pins" or a new "horizon line" for the air line. Some of the other businesses in town would also help provide entertainment for these vacationing children. Kids that we had sent off earlier would return from Chet's Hardware store saying that the clerk at Chet's wanted to know if we wanted the 3" or the 5" size retainer pins.

◆ One morning, a young girl and her brother showed up at the airline office counter with a rock picked up from the beach. It was a smooth brown rock and the young boy asked enthusiastically; *"Hey mister, is this rock worth any money?"* while his sister listened skeptically. We examined his newly found treasure and carefully showed it around the office. Not wanting the young boy to lose face in front of his sister, one of the dock boys in the office said excitedly; *"It looks like a Rustic Mucker, and a brown one at that!"*

The duo were then instructed to check with the Catalina Island Museum to verify the value of the found stone and off they went enthusiastically. It was late in the afternoon before we saw them again. They were obviously very tired from walking all day as they had been shuttled from one Rustic Mucker verification station to another. I am sure that the sister and brother slept very well that night and the parents were probably happy, too.

◆ Dock boys themselves were not immune from being targets for some of the mirth. One dock boy in particular was infamous for dating — or at least trying to date — girls in their early teens. Most dock boys were in their early 20's. This 20 year old dock boy was targeting the younger girls and we were determined to put a little "crimp in his style." When he became especially infatuated with one young girl who was staying on the island for the summer — it looked serious. To remedy this, we took out an ad in the — at that time — the one and only town newspaper that her parents were sure to see. I don't remember the exact text of the ad but it named him and, it read something like "Congratulations on your 25th birthday."

The Nights of Avalon

Dock boys liked to party. We had parties on the golf course — tee parties, we had parties at the Wrigley mausoleum, parties up and down the coast, and we had Chimes parties. The 4th of July holiday in Avalon bay traditionally features about four consecutive nights of fireworks launched from Casino Point. The view from the Chimes Tower on the hillside near Casino Point during these shows is a very close second to what Grace Kelly and Cary Grant saw on the French Riviera in the movie *To Catch a Thief*. Naturally, there were dock boy rules for celebrating this holiday spectacle. The rules had two parts. First, we needed to take a different girl to the fireworks show each night — no repeat girls. Second, we needed a new "tapper" each night — tappers were a newly introduced packaging for beer. The

This Catalina Air Lines company party was held at the Malibu Inn in Avalon. Dick and Nancy Probert are at right.

shape of the aluminum container was like that of a full size beer keg but they were smaller and held about a gallon of beer. Each night, to view the show, we would take our new date, a new tapper, and hoist everything over the tall barbed wire fence that guarded the Chimes Tower from trespassers. At night, large spotlights illuminate the Tower, and they had to be dealt with to keep from spoiling our view. I still have my windbreaker with the hole burned in the lining from when my twin brother laid it over one of the lights. Those were magical times.

Many of our parties were oriented around boats or boat trips. The trips down the coast at night were high times that featured bonfires, singing, beer, and hotdogs. These were sometimes capped by a return through a calm ocean that sparkled with iridescent algae, and frequently you were accompanied by an escort of flying-fish. In addition to the airline dock boy boat parties, other groups put on parties as well. One such party was held by a group calling itself the Balboa Punting and Sculling Society. This group knew how to throw a party. The first time that we heard of them they had placed a large boat on a railroad flatcar and partied all the way from Los Angeles to Palm Springs. When they came to Catalina they placed a full sized railroad car on a barge and partied all the way across the San Pedro Channel. For their return trip to the mainland however, the seas were too rough and a large group of them showed up at the airline office—still drunk and somewhat disorderly—trying to return to Los Angeles. Most of them took the steamer.

Another boat that showed up in Avalon bay was a Canadian submarine. It was moored just outside the harbor for a couple of days and we had much enjoyment interacting with the crew. They were a jolly lot just like us—young, mostly single males, wanting to party. After work one night, a few dock boys were in the John B Bar watching the piranha feeding in a tank located above the backlit shelves of beverage bottles behind the bar. In those days such activities were accepted and, besides, the John B had many charms to attract the random dock boy or sailor. Next to the tank, they had an 18" tall, battery powered Frankenstein monster doll that would growl, gesture, and then after a few seconds, his pants would fall down to his ankles. While enjoying the ambiance of the bar with some of the submariners, the front door opened, followed by a loud roar erupting from the sailors seated all around us. We looked quickly at the entrance to see what had caused the commotion. It was a single shore patrol sailor complete with uniform, arm band, and night stick. He was completely "snockered."

Immediately he was warmly greeted by his shipmates and escorted to our table where he was plied with even more drink. It appears that the custom, for these sailors at least, was to treat whoever had the shore patrol duty to unlimited drinks. In so doing, the sailors on shore leave had a duty that they looked forward to performing, and the shore patrol officer never had to arrest anybody.

Of all the parties that I remember, our own Catalina Air Lines company party stands out. Once each year, Dick Probert would hold a gathering on the island for all of the airline personnel. A suitable site would be selected. One year it might be the Zane Grey Pueblo, or the Malibu Inn, or the Catalina Country Club—any location where all employees could celebrate in style. The evening would begin with the Sikorsky flying to Avalon at dusk, bringing the staff from both Long Beach harbor and the Long Beach airport. Pilots, wives, station personnel, mechanics, reservation agents, ramp agents and dock boys all came. Upon docking 881 would disgorge its cargo of employees wearing their evening finery. The Sikorsky would be locked up at the dock for the night and off we would go for dinner, dancing, and drinking. The next morning reversed the procedure with a dawn departure scheduled so that the station personnel from the mainland could get back to ready their respective bases for the first flight out.

With her sister ship N329 attached to her mooring (these moorings were called "the hook" by the dock boys), N328 sits waiting at the seaplane floats in Avalon bay for her next load of passengers to be flown to Long Beach airport. Note the canvas ballast bags ready for use near the bow—they weighed 50 lbs apiece. This photograph was taken about 1965.

Epilogue

Combining the romantic island setting with classic aircraft and real-life pilot heros, the job of a dock boy in Avalon was stimulating. Sometimes strenuous, sometimes dangerous and challenging—it was always exciting—you never really knew what was going to happen next. Group unity, teamwork, and camaraderie existed along with a tremendous sense of pride and loyalty in the group that you simply cannot find in most relationships—then or now. Working as a dock boy in Avalon was a rare example of a job where co-workers would take time on their only day-off to come down to the office just to see what was going on.

All of us are fellow travelers in time—who travel in parallel with one another and effect many others' lives. By outlining the careers of the unique collection of individuals in this book, I have attempted to share their positive effects. The many island airlines of the last century with their varied aircraft painted in different color schemes, the water pilots with their individually fascinating backgrounds, and all of their supporting personnel have produced some beautiful colors for the tapestry of our society.

We all celebrate the now vanished sights, sounds, and people from the *"Golden Age of Aviation."* No memory from that time is more revered than that of the seaplanes and their pilots.

Bibliography

Angle, Paul M.
Philip K. Wrigley: A Memoir of a Modest Man. Chicago, IL: Rand McNally & Company, 1975

Allen, Oliver E.
The Airline Builders. Time-Life Books, 1981

Robert Allen Productions (video tape)
Catalina's Aviation History. Catalina Island Museum Society, Inc, 1988

Allward, Maurice
Seaplanes and Flying Boats. New York, NY: Dorset Press, 1981

Blair, Charles
Red Ball in the Sky. New York, NY: Random House, Inc., 1969

Davies, R.E.G.
Airlines of the United States Since 1914. Washington, DC: Smithsonian Institution Press, 1998

Farmer, James H.
Celluloid Wings: Impact of the Movies on Aviation: Blue Ridge Summit, PA, 1984

Gandt, Robert L.
China Clipper: The Age of the Great Flying Boats. Annapolis, MD: Naval Institute Press, 1991

Jablonski, Edward
Seawings: The Romance of the Flying Boats. Garden City, NY: Doubleday and Co. Inc., 1972

Knott, Richard C., Captain, USN
The American Flying Boat. Annapolis, MD: Naval Institute Press, 1979

Lawson, Robert and Tillman, Barrett
World War II US Navy Air Combat. Ann Arbor, MI: Lowe & B. Hould Publishers, 2002

Mizrahi, Joe
Air Classics Magazine (Vol. 3, No. 5) - *A Survey of the Planes That Put Grumman in the Catbird Seat of Naval Aviation*, May, 1967

New England Air Museum (video tape)
The Queen of the Sky. New England Air Museum, 2001

Overholt, Alma
The Catalina Story. Avalon, California: Edited and updated by Jack Sargent, curator, Catalina Island Museum: The Island Press, 1976
The Flight to Catalina - The Play Isle of the Pacific, Speed Magazine - August, 1930

Pember, Harry
Sikorsky VS-44 Flying Boat. Stratford, CT: Flying Machines Press, 1998

Rae, John B.
Climb To Greatness, The American Aircraft Industry, 1920–1960. Cambridge, MA: The MIT Press, 1968

Rosenthal, Lee
Catalina Tile of the Magic Isle. Sausalito, CA: Windgate Press, 1992
Catalina In the Movies. Sausalito, CA: Windgate Press, 2003

Serling, Robert J.
Legend and Legacy: The Story of Boeing and its People. New York, NY: St. Martin's Press, 1992
The Only Way to Fly: The Story of Western Airlines. New York, NY: Doubleday, 1976
When the Airlines Went to War. New York, NY: Kensington Publishing Corp, 1997

Sikorsky, Igor
The Story of the Winged S: New York, NY: Dodd, Mead & Company, 1938

Tucker, Albert S. J. Jr.
Pacific Clipper - The Untold Story. Lexington, VA: The News-Gazette Print Shop, 2001

White, William S.
Santa Catalina Island: Its Magic, People & History. Glendora, CA: White Ltd. Editions, 1997

Bibliography

Web Sites

Boeing Aircraft Company
www.boeing.com

Experimental Aircraft Association
www.eaa.org

Lockheed Martin Corporation
www.lockheedmartin.com

New England Air Museum
www.neam.org

Northrop - Grumman Aircraft Corporation
www.northropgrumman.com

Santa Catalina Island Chamber of Commerce
www.catalina.com

Santa Catalina Island Company
www.scico.com

Sikorsky Aircraft Corporation
www.sikorsky.com

National Air & Space Museum
www.nasm.si.edu

WEB sites dedicated to Grumman Gooses
www.catalinagoose.homestead.com
www.goosecentral.tripod.com
www.grummangoose.com

For additional information, set your WEB browser to search for any of the following: Donald W. Douglas; Flying Boats; Leroy Grumman; Grumman Goose; Dick Probert; or Igor Sikorsky.

About the Author

David Johnston was born in Los Angeles, California one week before the attack on Pearl Harbor. He graduated from El Camino College and California State University at Long Beach where he earned a degree in history. To help pay for college, he worked from 1962 to 1968 for Catalina Air Lines. He started working in Avalon Bay on the seaplane floats wrestling luggage, mail, boats, and aircraft—eventually becoming the Station Manager in Avalon. He also worked as the assistant Station Manager for Aero Commuter Airlines at Los Angeles International airport. In 1997, he planned, organized, and helped run the Catalina Island Seaplane reunion for seaplane pilots, airline personnel, and the general public.

As the song says, "I found my love in Avalon," David met his wife Janet on Catalina Island while he was working for Catalina Air Lines. Janet worked at Eric's Hamburger Stand at the land end of the green Pleasure Pier. Janet and Dave have one son, Greg, who took his first airplane ride in a Grumman Goose to Catalina Island at about age three months. Dave and Janet now reside in Oregon, where he is a computer instructor at Umpqua Community College, and he owns his own computer consulting business. He is a licensed pilot.

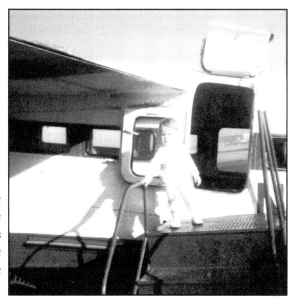

The author's son Greg, exits from an Catalina Air Lines Grumman Goose at Long Beach airport in 1967.